Iris Mu
"Com

Liz Dexter

Copyright © 2017 Liz Dexter

All rights reserved.

ISBN: 1974249646
ISBN-13: 978-1974249640

DEDICATION

Dedicated to my long-suffering husband Matthew and fans and scholars of Iris Murdoch everywhere.

CONTENTS

1.0 Introduction 1

2.0 Literature Review 9

3.0 Research Aims, Definitions and Methodology 51

4.0 The Reading Group Project 71

5.0 The Book Groups Project 99

6.0 Results and Discussion 103

7.0 Conclusions 143

Appendix: The Reading Group Themes 151

Appendix: The Book Group Questionnaire 153

Appendix: The Book Group Casts the Film 160

About the Author and Acknowledgements 161

Bibliography 163

1.0 INTRODUCTION

1.1 The very beginnings

I was introduced to the novels of Iris Murdoch (along with those of Virago-published and other luminaries such as Anita Brookner, Elizabeth Taylor and Barbara Pym) by a neighbour who acted as a sort of balance to the conformative, conservative (with a capital and lower-case 'c') and consumption-driven milieu in which I grew up. In a land of not speaking to the neighbours and never showing difference, she knitted, brewed beer, made her own ice cream, had a pressure cooker, grew all of her own vegetables and, most importantly, made her bookshelves available to the local children, with a hint of guidance here and there but no rules or strictures. I devoured *A Severed Head* first – what would I have made of that as a sheltered, only child attending a girls' grammar school, I often wonder. She instilled in me a life-long love of the novels of Iris Murdoch.

This was in the mid-to-late 1980s. From then on, having devoured the back catalogue, I anxiously awaited the publication of each new novel (in paperback) and spent my pocket money on amassing the full run of novels. I continued this practice, of course, right up until the 1995 publication of *Jackson's Dilemma*, and I also periodically read through the novels in order.

In 2008, it struck me that I had not re-read every single one of the novels in publication order, although I had enjoyed, for example, taking *The Philosopher's Pupil* on a Levantine holiday and reading it in the reception area of a Turkish hammam. I was living in Birmingham and had gathered a group of bookish friends, so when I decided to re-read the novels, I recruited some friends to read them alongside me. We were reading a novel every month (later changed to one every two months) and discussing them in detail in an online group I had set up, relating them to themes and looking at the literature on each book as we went.

This was the context in which I joined the Iris Murdoch Society and plucked up the courage to attend my first of the society's conferences, in 2010

1.2 Background to the research

In September 2010, I attended the Iris Murdoch Society Conference in Kingston (UK). Although I have a BA (Hons) in English Language and Literature and a Postgraduate Diploma in Library and Information Studies, I am not a working academic, and I attended the Conference as an 'Independent Scholar'. I expected to feel out of my depth and not 'academic' enough; however, I received a very warm welcome and there was a great deal of interest in my Iris Murdoch Reading Group. Many comments revolved around the pleasure the other delegates took in the idea that a) I was there under my own steam, not being an official academic, and b) people were reading Murdoch's novels out of their own interest. Ordinary people. 'Common readers', even.

I was actively encouraged to use the book group as

a springboard for a piece of research, which I could then apply to present on at the next Iris Murdoch Society Conference in September 2012. I came back from the Conference full of enthusiasm for this, and, once I had cleared it with the group, I began to formulate a set of questions which I could ask the group and which could form the basis of a short study which I could present to the Society in one form or another.

As I did this, the thought struck me that I could widen this research to look at whether Iris Murdoch would be a good subject for book groups in general. My attention had been drawn to the selection of reading material by book groups through my membership of a few groups over the years, and through my awareness of schemes such as the Richard and Judy Book Group. These seemed to concentrate on new and prize-winning novels: having drawn such pleasure from my reading of mid-20th century writers, I wondered if these would be as good for book groups as the latest recommendation or prize-winner.

I therefore decided to undertake a second line of research, into whether Iris Murdoch's novels would be suitable candidates for book groups.

1.3 The research

I conducted the two strands of my research concurrently from October 2010 through 2012, alongside working full and part time in a library and starting and running a small business. I asked the Iris Murdoch Reading Group the questions in two sections, one when we were still finishing the project, and the other when we had read all of the books. Simultaneously, I formulated and piloted the book group questionnaire, recruited book groups, sent out the questionnaire and received copies back.

Although not allied formally to any academic institution, I aimed to produce as academically rigorous a piece of work as I could, within the time and institutional constraints. I will therefore discuss my methodology and justify the research to the same standards as a Master's thesis. My ideas are all my own: I recruited a group of academics to read through the text at the end (two Iris Murdoch scholars and a social scientist).

1.4 The structure of the study

As befits an academic study, I will first conduct a review of the literature on the subject of book groups, with particular reference to their demographic make-up, their methods of choosing books (although this will not play a large role in my own research) and their definitions of what makes a 'good book group read', on Reception Theory, and on the book chosen to be read by the book groups: *The Bell*. I then outline my methodology, including my reasons for choosing the particular methodology and research instruments used, a description of those research instruments, and a note on ethics and confidentiality. There follows a case study of the Iris Murdoch Reading Group, including information on the members, their opinions of the books, and their reaction to the experience as a whole. Several important points are made here, including a discussion of whether Iris Murdoch is a good subject for book groups, which links in to the Book Groups research on *The Bell*. I then discuss my research with 25 book groups scattered around the UK and across the globe. The results of the questionnaires from my Book Groups are then given, with both qualitative and quantitative information drawn from the groups participating. This is then discussed with reference to the literature review, looking at how the groups match with groups discussed in former studies (to give this study validity and generalisability) and whether the criteria for 'a good book group read' also match those found in other studies. Some discussion of the differences between the 'ordinary readers'' thoughts on the book in question and those of academics will also tie in with my concentration on reception theory. I then draw conclusions from the study as a whole and offer the limitations and possibilities for future research.

1.5 Conclusion

I have discussed the background to the study and

highlighted the fact that I am not aligned to an academic department but made purely out of my own interest. However, I do have academic credentials of my own, and try as far as possible to make this study academically rigorous. I try to follow standard academic practice in the underpinnings behind and structure of my research. I have then outlined the content discussing my own group and book groups reading either all or one of Iris Murdoch's novels.

2.0 LITERATURE REVIEW

2.1 Introduction

In this chapter, I will briefly review the literature on the topics of book groups, including their demographics and what makes a good book group read, the literature on Reception Theory, and the literature on *The Bell*. The aim of this section is firstly to enable me to check whether the single reading group and the 25 book groups in my study conform to general findings on book groups in terms of demographics and ideologies, so making my results and conclusions generalisable across book groups; secondly, to explain something of the theoretical underpinnings of my research project in general; and thirdly to provide something of a contrast (or comparison) between 'professional' critical readings of the novel under discussion, other 'amateur' readings (drawn from personal input and also reviews from a book discussion site) and the opinions of my 25 book groups.

2.2 Review of literature on book groups

Book groups have been a popular field of study over the past decade or so, and a rich literature has built up about them. As Hartley (2001) describes, "[t]he powerful and distinctive engine of the reading group movement" (p. ix) has arisen in recent decades. Many of the studies are American in origin and several exist which examine the phenomenon of Oprah Winfrey's television book club (now defunct),[1] although there are no full-length monographs on the British Richard and Judy phenomenon (now moved from television to an online medium but still going strong). Book groups themselves have been flourishing for centuries but are hugely popular now, in what might be a backlash against a world lived increasingly online (although online book groups certainly exist and flourish and, for example, my own reading group communicated via a Yahoo group). I would like to make the assumption that you, the reader, either belong to a book group or know several, even many, people who do; they are woven into our culture, with books being written about them and television series featuring them (Noble, 2010; The Book Group, 2002).

In this section, I will concentrate on demographics, because one of the best ways of ensuring the validity and generalisability of sociological / ethnographical research of this kind is to check that the demographics of the groups under examination match those in the general literature. This means that other features of the groups are likely to match, too and any generalisations are more likely to hold true. My book group research and my case study look at the question of what makes a good book group read and whether Iris Murdoch's books fall into that category. I will also look briefly at the books that book groups choose, as this addresses my interest in introducing a mid-20th century author in to the book group choice mix. However, I do not go into depth on the methods that book groups use to make their choices, even though there is a wealth of literature on this topic and my book groups themselves were often eager to explain this aspect to me. This area was omitted as not being directly relevant, although it may well have a bearing on what books are chosen.

2.2.1 Book group studies and methodology

I will introduce some ideas about researching book groups at this stage, as I have found some explanations of how researchers recruited their groups. Hartley (2001), author of what is still the seminal work on book groups, surveyed 350 groups in the UK out of her approximation of 50,000 groups in existence at that time. (It appears that most other sources have found this figure and use it to date. A search for the current number of UK book groups yielded this figure quoted in a variety of resources (and not always referenced) on dates from 2001 to 2013, for example Viner, 2013.) Hartley contacted groups via the press, magazines, Wikipedia and word of mouth (p. ix). She received long, detailed and careful replies (p. ix). Long (2003) took a case study approach, looking at a few groups in the Houston area in depth. Because the area was not of such interest to academics at the time she was writing, she had to take a qualitative approach in general, rather than a quantitative one, as book groups were still almost "underground" (p. xii). She interviewed 47 women's book groups using a questionnaire.

Usefully, Long (2003) also experimented with asking her book groups to read something out of their norm, in this case a Jane Austen novel, and recorded their reactions.

2.2.2 The functions of book groups

Long (2003) quotes Martha Nussbaum (1990) in talking about how reading fiction helps readers to cultivate an ethical sensibility. Book group members in the literature talk about having their own time (for example women with busy family lives having something that is just theirs) and the companionship that groups bring. Hartley (2001) reports that they give much-needed intellectual challenge.

2.2.3 Book groups and demographics

Most of the literature on book groups agrees that they are mainly composed of women in their middle years. Indeed, some studies, such as Long (2003) chose to concentrate only on women's book groups. I have included this research in this literature review because, as we will see in future chapters, many of my 25 book groups (and indeed my own reading group) are composed solely of women, or have at most a scattering of men (it should be noted here that there are men-only reading groups; however, as none of my groups fell under that category, I have not included direct demographic research on what turns out to be a minority in this study).

Gender and age

Hartley (2001) found that 69% of her 350 UK-based groups were all-female, with 4% all-male and 27% mixed. With striking similarity, Long (2003) found that 64% of her general sample of American book groups consisted solely of women, 3% solely of men, and 33% were mixed. The longer a group in

Hartley's (2001) study had been in existence, the greater the mix of ages: but one third of her groups had all members in their 40s and one third at 50 plus; 12% had a wide age span, for example from 27 to 84 years old. Her oldest groups included members in their 80s and 90s.

Education and work

Studies which included information on the highest level of education recorded this in different ways. Eighty-eight per cent of Hartley's (2001) groups contained members with higher education qualifications, while Long (2003) recorded that in her groups, 21% of members had a Master's or advanced post-graduate degree, 23% had done some post-graduate work, while 25% had a degree as their highest qualification.

Hartley (2001) records that 67% of her groups had over half of their members in paid work.

Socio-economic status

Long (2003) states that membership of book groups tends to be drawn from pre-existing groups or people of similar socio-economic backgrounds (p. 61). Her groups rarely included anyone not college-educated.

2.2.4 How groups form

Hartley (2001) found that her book groups tended to form from special interest groups or groups of fans (p. 2). She specifies library groups, bookshop, Wikipedia and University of the Third Age (U3A) as well as *Mail on Sunday*-inspired groups (p. 16). In fact, a gay group based at the Waterstone's bookshop in Earl's Court were described as reading *The Bell*! However, the vast majority were what she terms 'neighbourhood groups' composed of people living in proximity and groups of friends (p. 14). Long (2003) found that groups came together because of shared ethnicity (for example, a group of Jewish women), background (college students), or life stage (for example, women with young children). Fifty-six out of her original 77 groups grew up through informal groups which were not work / church etc. related.

Hartley (2001) checked the size of her groups and found that 77% had 6-10 members, while 27% had 11-15 members.

2.2.5 Choosing books

Hartley (2001) found that her groups read alternating modern and classic books. Long's (2003) women's groups also read a mixture of classic and contemporary fiction and non-fiction (p. 84). They had in general, "A thirst for general and intellectually challenging reading" (p. 94) which needed to be fulfilled by the books chosen by the group. In a new development noticed by Long (2003), some of her groups had started to be influenced by the Oprah book club in choosing their books, as the television personality offered an alternative to the literary canon (p. 206): this implies that the groups require guidance in their choosing, whether in the form of tradition or a leader of some kind. This might suggest a reason for the higher take-up of my project than I'd expected, as someone undertaking an academic study could be considered to be an 'authority' in some way: if I thought it was worth their reading the book, then it was worth their doing so. Hartley's (2001) groups mentioned classics and prize-winners, the literary prize being another form of 'authority', although her study pre-dated the Richard and Judy book club phenomenon.

Farr (2008) identifies a feminist shadow tradition, outside the canon, off which women's reading groups have fed. While this not of immediate relevance to the work and author studied here, it does feed into ideas on Reception Theory, as will be discussed later on, in respect of an undermining of critical reactions. Farr also discusses a move in Oprah's book group from classics to contemporary best-sellers. It had an all-classics format from 2003-05 before returning to the contemporary best-sellers, although no specific reason for this is recorded (Farr, 2008, p. 5).

2.2.6 What makes a good book group read?

Long's (2003) groups found that it was most important to find books that generated "good discussions" (p. 114) and Hartley's (2001) groups took this for granted, outlining what made for a good discussion (p. 74) and mentioning that the book must provoke a good debate. In deciding whether something was 'discussable', Long's (2003) groups relied on the hegemony of the 'canon' and the evaluation of professionals and reviewers (p. 118). Top of the hierarchy were classics, followed by contemporary 'serious' fiction and non-fiction (biography, history, science, philosophy), then 'good' best-sellers such as James Michener, and finally genre fiction. They were led by literary awards and annual lists of notable books (p. 120), not so much the bestseller lists (p. 122). Long's group did mention that a book perceived as one of the 'best' might not be a good discussion book, i.e. if everyone agrees on their opinion of the book as being good and there is no actual discussion.

Quality

Long (2003) comments that for her groups, literary quality, particularly evidenced in 'good' writing (in terms of grammar, etc.) was important.

Themes and morals

Long's (2003) groups said that they liked books that have a moral balance or instruction (p. 149), but resisted a purely academic viewpoint (p.149).

Characters

Long's (2003) groups found that a satisfying discussion came, "when readers find the imagined worlds of a novel to be believable ... Characters whom readers can identify with and learn from appear to be most central to this process" (p. 151). They had a complex relationship with the characters in the books they read, but it involved recognition and closeness (p. 152).

Plot

Hartley's (2001) groups were interested in plot, although it was not the foremost reason for a book being a good book group read. They liked something with a mystery or conundrum (p. 74). The ambiguity and possible interpretations were what was key and most interesting here.

Challenge

Hartley (2001) found that her groups appreciated a book they would not necessarily have read without the group (p. 77). However, they liked to be able to relate to the book (see the section on personal reaction), i.e. not too far from their own experience, for example they did not like very foreign books (p. 76). Long's (2003) book groups enjoyed something that was different or something they could learn from (p. 177).

Personal reaction

Hartley (2001) found that for her groups, personal

reaction and empathy were most important: "The premium is on empathy, the core reading-group value. This empathy can go three ways: reader-character, author-character, and between all the readers in the room" (p. 132). In fact, one of her groups mentioned engagement in relation to Iris Murdoch's work: she records, "[e]ngagement is a key consideration for many groups in our survey" with one stating, "[u]nable to relate Doris Lessing's *Love Again* to our own experience" and another, "[w]e could not identify or sympathise with the characters in Iris Murdoch's novels" (p. 133). Long's (2003) groups stated that they were looking for "a reading experience that is personally significant and enduring" (p. 130), so a personal pleasure as well as a literary / intellectual one. Farr (2008) agrees, talking at length about 'affect': "Readers are drawn to literature's affect. They value novels they can take personally, novels that can speak to, challenge or transform their lives, novels that entertain them with lively stories or call them into political or social awareness, even action" (p.

3). In fact, according to Rooney (2005), Oprah in her book club *only* allowed a superficial reading, concentrating on how the book related to the lives of the readers personally, "More to do with the self-help narrative of her show itself" (p. 28). Hartley (2001) reflects this, too, stating that the need for a personal relationship with the book and the ability for the reader to apply their knowledge and experience to what they were reading has led to, "the reading-group preference for realism and for characters that readers can believe in" (p. 135).

Wider application

Long (2003), when discussing the history of the book group, talks about how the groups demonstrated that "a nuanced identification can lead group members to personal insights and encourage groups toward critical appraisals of the social order" (p. xviii). As just discussed, Farr (2008) mentions a side-effect of novel-reading on readers: it can "call them into political or social awareness, even action" (p. 3), and Hartley (2001) also mentions that the book is "expected to speak about the world, and the world (reading-group observation and experience) is brought to bear upon the book," in what she describes as an "open" relationship (p. 135) which can then open doors to other worlds. She describes the act of reading in book groups as "embedded reading, where the book thrives in a live cultural and social environment" (p. 138).

Other

Two other important guidelines for Long's (2003) groups were availability in paperback (this is actually to do with price) and local availability (p. 116). I am not now sure whether the impact of Amazon will have reduced this last requirement: I did advise my groups that copies of *The Bell* were available at a low price on the books website, feeding off this research. The provision of discussion notes was important to some of Hartley's (2001) groups.

2.2.7 Reading a new book

I was able to find in Long's (2003) study a discussion of asking groups to read a different kind of book from their normal reads and recording their reaction to it. She gave three groups a Jane Austen novel to read, and found that "both stylistically and substantively, these books were so different from what these book group members were used to that the books proved inaccessible even to willing readers" (p. 180). The groups tried to reframe the distance in terms that they felt familiar with, for example, "She's very good on characterizations" (p. 182).

2.3 Review of literature on reading and Reception Theory

2.3.1 The value of reading

Long (2003) quotes Nussbaum (1990) in talking about how reading fiction helps readers to cultivate an ethical sensibility. Newton (1995) says that encountering a book is like encountering and engaging with a person – but that you have to understand literary criticism to engage fully. However, as we will see, Reception Theory and my own readers undermine this assertion. Long (2003) herself takes exception to the way in which these writers are only concerned with canonical ethics rather than individual response: in her world-view, there is no 'right way' of reading a book.

2.3.2 Reading groups undermining the canon and academy

Farr (2008) discusses the way in which women's reading groups have tapped into a feminised shadow tradition, outside the canon: I am not sure that I agree with the term 'feminised', but their work in undermining the canon and critics is interesting here: "When readers were reduced to tears reading Stowe or Dickens, that was, for them, a sign of a good novel. For the critics, it was a mark of inferiority" (p. 3). Rooney (2005) has something to say about Oprah's book club in particular and the critics: "The majority of texts were of a higher quality than many critics would have us believe" (p. xii) but undermines this herself by agreeing with Farr: "Generally speaking, the majority of literature customers choose to praise and purchase reflects values that are a far cry from the ones held by those more ostensibly in the know" (p. 2). Farr goes on to say, "The meaning of texts … is defined not by the words themselves but by the community of readers who construct that text" (p. 5), showing Reception Theory to be alive and well in book group research in the first decade of the 21st century. However, she goes on to quote Perry's assertion that the difficult nature of the classics meant, "Abandoning the egalitarian nature of book clubs for a more hierarchical lesson led by experts" (p. 119, quoted in Farr (2008) p. 7). But Rooney (2005) asserts that the Oprah book club proved that "there exists a far greater fluidity among the traditional categories of artistic classification than initially meets the eye" (p. 5).

It is also interesting that Long's (2003) groups rejected books that have a purely academic viewpoint (p.149), and Hartley (2001) quotes James Naughtie, who ran a Radio 4 Bookclub as saying that it is "a readers' conversation, not a critics' conversation" (p. 5). Hartley (2001) emphasises this point later in her study: "Reading groups are about reading in the community rather than the academy. Indeed, being non-academic may be part of their self-definition" (p. 138). Turner (2007) discusses Murdoch as being part of a 'nonce canon' of popular contemporary writers – "I propose that this 'nonce' canon involves critical acclaim that is both 'academic' ... and 'popular' (a wider reading public). Murdoch, most unusually in her era, spanned both" (p. 116), which could explain Murdoch's possible appeal to reading groups. However, 'nonce' canon books do not always make it into the main canon and thus gain the 'authority' that appeals to book groups.

2.3.3 Iris Murdoch undermining the canon and the academy

Iris Murdoch was not the biggest fan of the

academy. She is quoted in White (2014) as writing to Hal Lidderdale about Oxford academia: "The society gets me down in the long run tho! The donnishness of people, the cleverness – all the bleeding <u>intellectuals</u>. What a relief to board the London train and see all those spires disappearing" (p. 86; emphasis in original). She is quoted in the Introduction to Rowe (2007) as wishing her texts to be read outside the academy: she "wanted texts to be evaluated by the calm, open, judging mind of the intelligent experienced critic, unmisted as far as possibly by theory" (p. 2, quoting Conradi, p. 454). She was even stronger in an interview in *The Times* in 1964: "One never learns anything one doesn't know from critics" (Murdoch, 2003).

In her *Paris Review* interview, when Iris Murdoch was asked what effect she would like her books to have, she replied, "I'd like people to enjoy reading them. A readable novel is a gift to humanity. It provides an innocent occupation. Any novel takes people away from their troubles and the television set; it may even stir them to reflect about human life, characters, morals. So I would like people to be able to read the stuff. I'd like it to be understood too; though some of the novels are not all that easy, I'd like them to be understood, and not grossly misunderstood. But literature is to be enjoyed, to be grasped by enjoyment." Her ideal reader was described thus: "Those who like a jolly good yarn are welcome and worthy readers. I suppose the *ideal* reader is someone who likes a jolly good yarn and enjoys thinking about the book as well, thinking about the moral issues" (Meyers, 2003).

2.3.4 Reception Theory, Death of the Author and Reader-Response Theory

Reader-Response Criticism is the term used (for example by Abrams, 1993) for a group of theoretical positions which concentrate on the process of reading a literary text, turning a literary work into a process or "activity on the part of the reader" (p. 269).

Ricoeur (1981, quoted in Abrams, 1993) says that the author's meaning, once it is inscribed in a text, takes on a life of its own. This process of autonomisation takes place whenever speech is inscribed in a text. This means that the text now has an autonomous, 'objective' existence independent of the author. Ricoeur suggests that the hermeneutic task is to make Aristotle's writings our own. The "text is the medium through which we understand ourselves". Gadamer (1976b, quoted in Abrams, 1993) suggests that meaning does not reside in either the subjective feelings of the person interpreting it or the author's intentions; rather, meaning emerges from the engagement of reader and text. This process of critical engagement with the text is crucial.

While proponents of this idea differ in the details, they agree that the meaning of a text is the creation of the individual reader, so there is no 'correct' response to the text. They differ in the degree to which they will admit any constraints imposed by the text on their meaning. Iser (1978), for example, sees the text as imposing structures to which a response was invited, with the text almost in dialogue with the reader. The 'real reader' then imposes patterns gained from their outside experience, and is different from the 'implied reader' in the writer's mind who will respond only in the way in which they are invited to respond. This allows some readings to be rejected as misreadings. I would take a similar middle way on this, in that I am not sure that any type of reading can be imposed on any type of text, although my book group readers in fact in my view pushed at the constraints of *The Bell* and forced me and my audience to address an alternative view of some events in the book.

Michel Foucault and Roland Barthes reacted at a similar time to the work of the post-structuralists by announcing "the death of the author", denying the key function or role of the author as the foundation of all knowledge and determiner of the form and meaning of a text. This leaves the reader as the central figure in engaging with the text and creating its meaning. Stanley Fish (1974, quoted in Abrams, 1993) talks interestingly of the reader with "literary competence" who is an "informed reader" who can make special sense of a text. This informed reader sounds a lot like Virginia Woolf's common reader and my ordinary reader, in that they have a knowledge of literary forms and functions which inform their reading. He later expanded this idea to talk of "interpretive communities" made up of readers who share a set of assumptions which create the text among themselves.

Reception Theory was initiated by Hans Robert Jauss and was at its most popular in Germany in the 1970s (Jauss, 1971, cited in Abrams, 1993; Holub, 1984). It represents "A general shift in concern from the author and the work to the text and the reader" (Holub, 1984, p. xii). It is a type of Reader-Response Theory, but with a historical application; as Abrams explained, "its prime interest ... is not on the response of a single reader at a given time, but on the altering responses, interpretive and evaluative, of the general reading public over the course of time" (Abrams, 1993, p. 272). A given text thus possesses no fixed or final meanings, or value and attention is paid to the changes in meanings of texts over time.

2.3.5 Is Death of the Author and Reader-Response theory relevant today?

Although these theories are not now much discussed, having fallen out of favour, the thoughts behind them can be found threaded through popular culture. For example, singer Tracey Thorn (2015) has this to say regarding performance:

> at a concert, a singer may perform an emotional song while being actually very detached from the emotion. The listener, however, perceives the presence of strong emotion – so who has put it there? If the singer isn't conscious of feeling anything at the time, and is potentially just going through the motions, is emotion really present or is the listener imagining it? […] There is a wealth of your own personal meaning encoded within the song, and, in a way, the singer is completely extraneous to the experience you're having.

2.3.6 Murdoch and her own 'death' in her books

There are many examples to be found in Murdoch's

own words that she did not wish to be identified within her books (I accept that the irony is evident here). In an interview with Harold Hobson in 1962, she said, "I agree with Eliot that the artist's task is the expulsion of himself from the work of art" (Hobson, 2003, p. 7). In an interview with Bellamy in 1977, she expressed disdain for literary theory engaging with too much philosophy, leaning towards an idea of just reading the text: "I'm against the instruction into literary criticism of jargonistic philosophical theories. I don't think it helps. One has to keep a very open mind about literature and just look and respond to the work with one's whole self" (Bellamy, 2003, p. 52). She was open to people's different interpretations of her novels, to an extent (see below), commenting during a symposium on her work, "It's not surprising if people interpret a novel in different ways. And the author is very likely to be tolerant to different interpretations – or, at least I am, because I see a pattern in the book which I may have only partly realized, and which is mixed in with other patterns" (Todd, 2003, p. 180).

Murdoch expressed several times that it was important to her that people simply enjoyed reading her books; for example, "I am very pleased if people read my books and think what a good story, I want to know what is going to happen without bothering about any of the intellectual refinements which might be there, or the other things which might be there […] it is not like watching television, it is different, it is high consolation, and that's all right" (Bigby, 2003, p. 105), not minding if people do not, for example, work out who Mr Loxias is in *The Black Prince* (Todd, 2005, p. 187) and, more simply, "I would like the reader to see everything in the book. But I'm glad if people like those stories, it gives me pleasure, because stories are a very good way, you know, of getting away from one's troubles" (Brans, 2003, p. 166).

However, it is important to note that Murdoch also expressed that "a willingness to hand over the interpretation to the reader is another thing and I don't want to do the latter," referring to puzzles and mysteries or making things clear (Bigby, 2005, p. 105), so the death of the author is clearly not everything to her, and every text does not lie wide open for a range of interpretations, although she did also contradict this in a symposium: "Other interpretations I think would be mistaken, but of course this is just what the author thinks, and in the end it's persons other than the author who are going to decide what the work means" (Todd, 2005, p. 193).

2.4 Review of literature on reading Iris Murdoch and Iris Murdoch's The Bell

Iris Murdoch's novels and general critical reactions to them is too large a topic to be able to treat comprehensively here. Many books of criticism are available on this topic, as are books on Murdoch's friends' reactions to her books. Here I will concentrate on what was findable on general readers' reactions to Murdoch, then on a selection of viewpoints, academic and 'common', on *The*

Bell.

2.4.1 Critical reactions

2.4.1.1 Reading Iris Murdoch

Nicol (2007) in his chapter on *The Bell* but talking generally at this point, makes the comment that readers respond to the story in Murdoch's work: "Murdoch's status as supreme story-teller is at the heart of responses to her novels. Those who dislike her fiction object to a kind of excess – of which narrative excess is one of the most central features. Those who enjoy it are gripped by precisely this glorying in the constant twists and turns of plot" (p. 102). Turner (2007) also asserts that the foregrounding of narrative links the academic and popular fields, for example, discussing *Henry and Cato*, "The Greene-like violence of Henry has both a moral point and a drive which involved this reader at a surface level" (p. 118).

Turner (2007) quotes A.S. Byatt's assertion of 2003 that no one was reading Murdoch any more and the charm had worn off (p. 115). He mentions that Jan Morris felt she was becoming dated, the public began to tire of her around the publication of *The Message to the Planet*, and as the Young British Artists and Granta novelists took hold, reviewers took against her portrayals of what was seen as not the real world. Academic studies played a part in this, in that her books are not open to feminist readings, for example.[2]

Dooley (2003) backs up that our reading of Murdoch should not be influenced by our knowledge of her final years, quoting Robert Weil, John Bayley's American editor: "to pay too much attention to Murdoch's last years would be 'a horrendous trivialisation of a remarkable career'," (p. xxix), and although the book groups were aware of issues around her Alzheimer's and decline, it did not overwhelm all of their reactions.

2.4.1.2 Reading The Bell[3]

Nicol (2007) asserts the view of the reader in his discussion of *The Bell* in Rowe (2007): as soon as

Paul has recounted the story of the bell, we are looking for parallels, and expecting a death once it has tolled. Nick's suicide makes us choose between the rational and the irrational: is it a product of the curse or simple coincidence? Nicol states that we become involved in the text, mirroring the experience of the characters. This statement links more than many other writers to the reading experience of the book groups I have discussed above. Most of the other writers talk simply about themes, motifs, religious and artistic symbolism. Jean Kennard (1975, quoted in Soule, 1998) points out the existence of a "technical scene" in the lifting of the bell, which my original book group called "Complicated plans" and found in each book. Kennard describes the aim of such passages as being "so precise as to make readers realize how remarkable the world is," which goes further than the perception of the group (Soule, 1998, p. 252). Margot McCarthy (1968, cited in Soule, 1998, p. 253) speaks of the many pairings of contrasting characters (Dora and Michael, Noel and Paul, Nick and Toby, Nick and Catherine, and the two bells). This echoes the "Dualities / Pairs" theme found by my original book group.

Frank Baldanza (1974, cited in Soule, 1998, p. 243) discusses the themes, recurrent motifs and characters of the book and the symbolism of the bell, and finds the central contrast as being between the two leaders, James and Michael. Nick (evil) and Dora (innocent) provide two extremes. Marvin Felheim (1960, cited in Soule, 1998, p.247) during the early part of Murdoch's career concentrates on pairs of female characters in the novel, here Catherine and Dora, the withdrawn and independent. Dorothy Jones (1967, cited in Soule, 1998, p. 251) sees the novel as being about the contrast between pattern and contingency, with Michael seeing himself as a passive part of a divinely ordained pattern.

David Beams (1988, cited in Soule, 1998, p. 243-44) puts forward a new theory on the allegory of the novel, talking about the New Testament in a place of Old Testament lore and a dramatisation of the incarnation and resurrection (not something my readers touched upon). Daniel Majdiak (1972 cited in Soule, 1998, p. 254) finds it to be a parody of the contemporary Anglican ideals of T.S. Eliot. Elizabeth Dipple (1982 cited in Soule, 1998, p. 246) concentrates on the sacred and profane, seeing the characters through this lens. Deborah Johnson (1987, cited in Soule, 1998, p. 250) sees a feminist subtext to the novel, with symbols of female sympathy and examples of subjugation, with Dora expressing her repressed sexuality through ringing the bell. My readers expected feminism but found none.

It is Cheryl Bove's view (1993, cited in Soule, 1998) that James and Michael are at opposite ends of a spectrum of advice, with the Abbess at the centre with her realism. Dora learns from her experiences (Soule, 1998, p. 243). This agrees with Peter Conradi's (1986, cited in Soule, 1998, p.245) assertion about the Abbess taking a balanced view of both sides. He found Michael to be at the centre of the novel. Frances Hope had also back in 1964 (cited in Soule, 1998, p. 250) found the heart of the book as lying in the contrast between the two men's sermons.

Many writers have, as we have seen, touched on or discussed *The Bell* and A.S. Byatt's (1994) long chapter on the novel is one of the most well-known. Although mentioning her own reactions to, for example, the gipsy in *The Sandcastle*, she keeps her discussion to the literary theory, discussing the symbolism of the bell itself, the two central characters as she sees them, Dora and Michael, and the theme of repetition and religion. She mentions Michael as feeling he has corrupted the young (Byatt, 1994, p. 99) and that themes in Murdoch embrace both damaging the young and the resilience of youth, but makes no overt mention of paedophilia. She had earlier, in 1976, spoken of how Murdoch was trying to emulate 19th century novels in her free and formless characters who are able to work out their own destinies (Soule, 1998, p. 245).

David Gordon (1995) sees a structural irony in the contrast between Dora and Michael, both with an ordeal which they cannot complete, and sees Michael as being chastised for playing a role he cannot sustain.

Osborn (2014a) draws more overt conclusions on Michael's behaviour, writing of the reader's ability to challenge Michael's perspective (p. 87) and quoted Byatt's discussion of Michael's unreliability as a narrator. She highlights the exclusion of Nick's voice from the retrospective section of the novel as evidence that we can "[read] between the lines of [Michael's] memories" (p. 88) on "what amounts to the corruption of a minor" (p. 89). Gabriele Griffin had already in 1993 made a point of Michael's dreams confusing the reader as to what is real, prefiguring Osborn's and Byatt's discussion of him as an unreliable narrator. But at the other extreme, Packer (1977, cited in Soule, 1998, p. 225) speaks of Michael's love for Nick as being related to the Good, although not opening his heart, Dorothy Winsor sees Michael's love for Nick as being "protective" (Winsor, 1980, cited in Soule, 1998, p. 259), Diana Phillips (1991, cited in Soule, 1998, p. 255-6) also claims that Michael's imperfect love could have saved Nick, the "aggressor", with no whiff of corruption, and Hilda Spear (1995, cited in Soule, 1998, p. 257) sees Michael's life as illustrating the difficulty of reconciling the sensual and the spiritual.

All of the works discussed here are pieces of academic criticism, so will of necessity have different viewpoints to those of the "ordinary reader". It is worth noting their interest in themes, religion and laying out the characters according to patterns and continuums. When they do mention Michael's "corruption" of Nick, they do not push a reading of culpable paedophilia until we reach the most recent point of Osborn (2014a).[4]

2.4.2 Reactions of the common reader

Note here that Amazon and the Amazon-owned Goodreads website are known anecdotally not to be enthusiastic about quotation from their reviews, so I gained permission from Tim Spalding of LibraryThing (Spalding, 2012) to quote reviews from the librarything.com website. All reviews from book review websites or other online resources are referenced with the reviewer's name and the website. I also gathered personal opinions from some people who had become aware of my book groups project but did not themselves belong to book groups.

Reviewers on the LibraryThing range from writing long, detailed reviews to discussing authors whom Murdoch resembles. Many set out the plot rather than going much deeper, but several discuss the depth, complexity and quality of the writing. One member of one of my book groups crops up on here, mentioning the project and outlining her distaste for some dated references she considered racist and outmoded which she also mentioned in her feedback. They pull out themes of sexuality and religion, sometimes seeing the book through a modern lens and commenting that the characters' concerns seemed absurd. There is a celebration of

Murdoch's bravery and openness in writing about themes such as homosexuality at a time when that was illegal, and in a non-judgemental way. Only one reviewer mentions a theme of child abuse overtly, with most referring to a relationship or affair; this could be down to the site being public and reviews being linked to profile names.

2.5 Death of the author: review of literature on Iris Murdoch and legacy

Turner (2007) discusses how Murdoch had become, by 2007, an "Alzheimer's poster girl", which eclipsed the reputation of her novels (p. 120). However, in recent years there has been a flowering of academic discussion (for example at the Iris Murdoch Society Conference and other international conferences that have sprung up); Vintage have reissued her books and they are reputed to be selling well (Turner, 2007). Having said that, only *The Sea, The Sea* has an Amazon ranking of above 5000, and Turner still asserted that, "Evidence together confirms that Murdoch has slipped out of the 'popular' canon and become unfashionable" (p. 120). Books on Murdoch have concentrated both on her literary output (for example, Conradi, 2010) and personal experiences and relationships (Morgan, 2010), or both at the same time (Horner and Rowe, 2015; Martin and Rowe, 2010).

Pamela Osborn (2014b) spoke about the mourning of Murdoch in a paper presented at the Iris Murdoch Society Conference in 2014. She analysed the life writing on Murdoch presented by authors such as Conradi, Bayley, Morgan and Wilson and discussed how they show the uniqueness of personal mourning but also a feature of people building upon and discussing previous works of mourning. She asserted that mourning now is presented through biography, incorporating the dead into the lives of the survivors and their personal reactions.

2.6 Conclusion

I have reviewed the critics and common readers'

discussions on reading Murdoch, reading *The Bell* and her legacy. I will now go on to discuss the aims, definitions and methodology of the research itself.

3.0 RESEARCH AIMS, DEFINITIONS AND METHODOLOGY

3.1 Introduction

In this chapter I outline the aims and questions of the study as a whole, lay down some definitions and choices of theories to underpin the work, and then discuss my choice of methodology and research instruments, before outlining the construction and use of these instruments for collecting data.

3.2 Research aims

The main research aim is to discover whether the novels of Iris Murdoch are suitable candidates for selection by modern book groups, given their seeming reliance on modern and prize-winning books.

3.3 Research questions

The research questions chosen to answer the aims are as follows:

- Is Iris Murdoch, in general, still readable and enjoyable by the 'ordinary reader'?

- What constitutes a "good book group read"?

- Do Iris Murdoch books in general constitute "good book group reads"?

- Does *The Bell* in particular constitute a "good book group read"?

3.4 Definitions and choices

3.4.1 Reception theory

Having subscribed to the idea of 'Death of the Author' in my previous academic explorations, I am taking a 'Reception Theory' view of the reaction of readers to texts. Reception theory looks at the response of the reader to the text: it focuses on the reader's own individual response to the text, and how that response forms the meaning of that text for the reader, outside the academic or literary response to the text, and forming radically different meanings related to the cultural environment and knowledge of the reader themselves.

I see Reception Theory as giving a radical validity to the ordinary reader's response to the text, a validity which can be just as acceptable as the canonical academic response. This is a thread which has emerged in studies of book groups, maybe particularly precipitated by the 'Oprah phenomenon', whereby responses were centred deeply in people's personal experiences rather than being focused on literary matters or even merit.

Reception Theory has been further explained in the Literature Review chapter: here I am defining my terms and my theoretical underpinnings.

3.4.2 The 'Ordinary Reader'

It needs to be clarified here that I am not suggesting imposing a reading of Iris Murdoch novels onto the non-readers of this world. I originally called my suggested pool of readers the 'Common Reader', after Virginia Woolf's (1925) definition of an intelligent person who reads for pleasure but with some kind of purpose: "He is guided by an instinct to create for himself out of whatever odds or ends he can come by, some kind of whole – a portrait of a man, a sketch of an age, a theory of the art of writing." By definition, members of book groups are seeking discussion of the books they read, and reading them in a more aware and maybe even 'literary' way (however, see the discussion in the literature review about the ways of reading book group members impose upon their books).

The Common Reader is placed somewhere between the non-reader and the academic. My terminology, though, had to change: when I mentioned that I was looking for a reaction from the Common Reader to *The Bell*, two of the group leaders took exception to the phrase, and the term 'Ordinary Reader' was felt to be more appropriate.

To me, the two mean the same: the intelligent, not necessarily highly-educated, but 'active' reader, overtly interested in the text, its meaning (whether in general, or in relation to their own life) and its relevance (again, in general, or in relation to their own experience).

3.4.3 *The Bell* as representative novel chosen

In this section I will justify my choice of *The Bell* as the book the Book Groups participating in the study were asked to read.

I made my choice based on three areas: my own perception of the novels; the Iris Murdoch Reading Group's reaction to the novel; and the common reasons book groups in general give for choosing books to read. More information on this last will be found in the Literature Review.

My own perception of the novels led me to look at one of the earlier, rather than later novels. The later novels became very long and appeared more challenging, whereas *The Bell* is reasonably compact. It has a wide range of characters and issues, from religion to homosexuality. It is the novel by Murdoch with which I recommend interested readers to start.

The Iris Murdoch Group universally liked this novel and found it less threatening than other, later, novels. They stated that it has classic Murdochian themes and that she had settled into what they referred to as her style and milieu (as in groups of educated people who spend a lot of time discussing matters philosophical) by the time she wrote this work.

Book groups in general like a book which has a range of different characters with whom readers can identify, and strong themes which are ripe for discussion. They should be of reasonable size and easy and cheap to obtain. All of these ideas are explored in more detail in the Literature Review chapter. I checked availability of the book in both UK public libraries and on Amazon, and found good and cheap availability.

In addition, I noted that a TV adaptation was made of this novel in the 1980s, thus it is already deemed suitable for a wide audience.

As I was making the choice for book groups with this book, I wanted to match the kind of parameters they would normally choose. Some groups accepted the challenge straight away, while others put the book into the general group of books to choose from – all had some discussion as to whether to read this book. So it was important to me to choose a novel which was representative of Iris Murdoch's work as a whole, while fitting in to the general criteria book groups use to choose their reading matter.

3.5 Approaches and methodology

3.5.1 Approaches

I used an interpretivist approach, which claims that knowledge is socially constructed and that all kinds of information are valid (Thomas, 2009). This fits in with the Reception Theory which underpins my study as a whole. In the interpretivist approach, the world (or our reading of a text) is constructed by each of us in a different way (Thomas, 2009: p.75). There are no verifications or hypotheses involved; instead, the interpretation of the results springs from the results themselves.

My ontological assumptions were that readers create the meaning from their text and that readers in book groups wish to read books which fit in with their own ontological assumptions of what a good book group read is. I aimed to find out how this world works by building up a body of "thick description" (Geertz, 1975, cited in Thomas, 2009) and allowing my participants as much space as they need to narrate their own reactions to their experience and to the questions asked.

I took an ethnographical stance in this research, being involved in the case study as a participant as well as a researcher. I note here that some bias may be caused by my being involved in this study, and also in some of the book group leaders being personally known to me. However, the case study participants had been open and honest during our years of discussion, not pulling back from being negative about books they knew I liked, and it was noticeable that the comments from book groups where the leader knew me personally and those where they did not were very similar in tone and content, so I am not convinced that any researcher bias was present there.

3.5.2 Methodology choices

The interpretivist approach lends itself to a qualitative research methodology, finding out information via "words, thoughts and images" rather than "verification" (Thomas, 2009: p. 83). So using the classic qualitative research instruments of the case study and questionnaire allowed me to gather data that would inform a narrative of the opinions of the groups, mediated through the group leaders.

I applied some quantitative measures to draw out the demographic information, in order to compare it to that found in the literature and check whether my groups matched the previous findings on the make-up of book groups in general. I also use simple yes / no measures in order to be able to pronounce with clarity on the central question of the research: is Iris Murdoch a good candidate for book group book selection.

3.5.3 The case study

The sample for the case study was small and self-selecting, being formed from a group of people who were, by the time of the start of the study, almost all the way through a chronological reading of Iris Murdoch's novels. However, the fact that the project had almost finished meant that the discussions of the earlier books were not self-conscious, in regard to this study, and the tone and content of the discussions did not noticeably change once this research study had started.

A set of questions was formulated which was designed to find out about the participants' expectations of and experience of the process of reading and discussing Iris Murdoch's novels in publication order, as well as their thoughts on whether Iris Murdoch would be a good book group author. To minimise participant fatigue and to capitalise on their interest in the research project while acknowledging that the chronological reading had not yet finished, I split the questions into two parts, one applied a few months before the end of the reading project, and the other after it had finished. This worked well, although I had to issue several reminders to the participants, and one did not complete the second questionnaire (however, she had inadvertently answered some of the questions in this second questionnaire in her enthusiastic responses to the first part).

3.5.4 The Book Group questionnaire – formulation and pilot study

It is important when running a questionnaire to run a pilot study first on one or more groups, to ensure the validity, usefulness and comprehensibility of the questionnaire. As I was not initially expecting more than ten responses in total, I decided to run the questionnaire on one pilot group in the first instance.

I formulated the questions based on the research questions. The first section was about how the book group had formed, whether it was based around an original friendship, work or organisation group or had formed for the purpose of starting a book group, and the six most recent books the group had read. These questions were aimed at the book group leader (although some groups discussed these answers within the group too) and aimed at finding out the background to the group, giving me a way to compare the groups with those discussed in the previous literature. I then started the group questions with demographic questions on age, gender, ethnic group, highest level of education achieved and employment status. I did not ask a question about income, as some of the American studies did, as I did not feel this would be something the predominantly UK-based groups would be keen to answer. I felt it was more important to gain basic information from everyone, than detailed information from just some. As described in the ethics section below, I ensured that the groups could collect this information anonymously. The next set of questions asked about the book itself, then I asked what constituted a good book group read, and, finally, whether they would recommend *The Bell* to other individuals or book groups, and whether it made a good book group read. A final question allowed for any further comments.

Once this questionnaire had been formulated, I ran it on a pilot group. This was a book group to which I had belonged, and the leader was a personal friend: to avoid researcher bias I was not present when the idea of taking part in the research was floated, or when the vote was taken, and nor was I present when the discussion took place. I provided the group leader with some information on the background to the project which I subsequently used for all the groups. The set-up was identical to that planned for the other groups, in that I sent the questionnaire by email and it was returned to me in the same way.

Once Group Anax had gone through their questionnaire, I asked a final question: whether they had any comments on the questionnaire itself. There were no comments or criticisms from the group or group leader on the questionnaire or the process. I therefore did not change the questionnaire, and I was able to count Anax as my first full participant group as well as my pilot group.

3.5.5 The Book Group questionnaire – the final questionnaire

The remainder of the book groups were selected through an attempt at a 'snowball effect' and a necessary self-selection. I formulated a short statement about the research, and backed this up with a page on my website explaining the research in more detail. I then attempted to contact as many possible participants as possible by reaching out in the following ways:

- I emailed a large group of friends and asked them to pass the email on to anyone who had a book group or belonged to one (this spread well and recruited many of my participant groups, some at third or fourth hand)

- I had a notice inserted in a University newsletter which went out to all central administrative staff (this gained a couple of groups)

- The Iris Murdoch Society sent a mailing to all members – this recruited some groups and some academics who added a further level to the data I was able to obtain. I did not end up using material from the academic study groups as it fell awkwardly between the critics and ordinary readers, but did not add to either

- I posted on a Penguin books website discussion board – this gained no respondents

- I sent Tweets on Twitter to librarians who might be interested – this gained one group

3.6 Ethics

The ethical side of research is something that is heavily stressed by academic organisation. My ethical policy, revolving around anonymity, took two strands, corresponding to the two facets of my research.

3.6.1 The Case Study

Regarding the Case Study, I asked the other participants in the group, immediately upon deciding to undertake the research, whether they had any objections to my using the ideas and posts that we had generated within the Yahoo Group. I asked this within the Yahoo Group itself, but stressed that participants were free to email me in confidence. All of the members of the group gave me explicit, emailed permission to quote their words as posted to the group. I asked if they wished to remain anonymous. They all waived the right to anonymity and so I used their real names in the writing up of the Case Study. With regard to the two members of the group who did not eventually participate in the research questionnaires, I part-anonymised them by referring to them only by initials, and advised them that I would be doing this.

Although all discussions of the individual novels and their themes, and the initial discussion about this research study, were carried out within the 'public' arena of the Yahoo Group (this was a closed group, with membership by invitation only, so the public aspect only involved the other members of the group), I asked that the responses to the questionnaires be submitted to me individually, by email, meaning each set of responses was private at the time. Permission was explicitly given to quote from these responses, and the main reason for asking for them individually was to ensure that I received the respondents' own individual thoughts, not influenced by one another.

3.6.2 The book groups

Because I was collecting demographic data from the book group participants, it was important that I respected their anonymity and confidence. I therefore undertook the following processes:

I reassured the group leaders with whom I corresponded that only I would know their names and group details. I did this through the additional text I sent with the questionnaire, and also reassured them via email if necessary. I advise them that I would anonymise the group when writing about it.

As each completed questionnaire came in, I assigned the group a letter, consecutively from A. I actually found that this looked a little 'dry' and formal, and ended up assigning each group a name from an Iris Murdoch novel beginning with that letter.

I stressed that the gathering of demographic information, vital for part of my research but obviously sensitive, should be done anonymously within the group. After the experience of the first, pilot, group, I suggested using their method, which was to circulate slips of paper with the questions and collect them in an envelope. I wrote up this experience on a blog post and directed my other groups' attention to this.

3.7 Conclusion

This section has outlined the research aims, some definitions, the approaches and the methodology used in an attempt to make this study by an independent scholar match the quality of an academic work to as large an extent as possible given the circumstances and parameters involved. I now go on to discuss the Reading Group project, then the Book Groups project.

4.0 THE READING GROUP PROJECT: INTRODUCTION AND METHODOLOGY

In late 2007, I decided I wanted to re-read Iris Murdoch's novels in chronological order. I had done this before, but not since the late 1990s, and had only read the later three once each. Discussing this with a few friends, some local, and some web-based, we decided to form a reading group to read and discuss the books.

Fast forward to September 2010. We had got up to *The Philosopher's Pupil* by the time I attended the fifth Iris Murdoch Society Conference as an independent scholar. Talking to a few people at the event, I realised that there was a great deal of interest in these 'ordinary readers', who were reading the books because they wanted to, not because they had to, were studying them, or their academic career depended on it. I was encouraged to write up a case study of this group to share with the Society.

I then decided to go one better. As well as writing up a case study, I decided to recruit some book groups to read an Iris Murdoch novel, discuss it, and let me know whether it seemed to be a good book group read. As many of us, I am sure, do, I am forever pressing Murdoch books on unsuspecting readers, and this seemed a good opportunity to promote the books and to see whether a mid-century literary author could hold her own among the prize-winners and Oprah / Richard and Judy selections that seemed at a casual glance to be prevalent among book group reads.

4.1 The reading group

4.1.1 Members

The original participants in the group were Liz (me), Gill and Ali, who live in the same city, and Audrey, who lives in Scotland. Ali, Gill and I met through BookCrossing (a group which engages in leaving books for people to find, but also encourages meet-ups) in 2005 when I moved to this area, and Audrey and I had known each other via an online book group, since around 2004. Audrey dropped out of the group around the time we read *Bruno's Dream* due to pressures of work and personal issues, and did not join in the discussions on the case study.

We had three members join the group at a later stage. One lady, who I met through LibraryThing (an online website for cataloguing personal collections of books, which also has group chat facilities) discussion groups, joined us for *Bruno's Dream* and *A Fairly Honourable Defeat* but dropped away after that and very unfortunately passed away a year or so later.

Lucy joined in January 2010 and read from *Nuns and Soldiers* onwards with the group. Once she had joined the group, she read most of the others (under her own steam and not in sequence), except for *The Red and the Green*, and started, but did not finish, *The Flight From the Enchanter* and *The Black Prince*. I originally befriended Lucy via the LibraryThing discussion groups. Sam is another friend from our BookCrossing activities in our home town; she was a less active discusser but read along where she could and looked at our posts, and she decided to join us fully for the last three.

I was a qualified librarian in my late 30s who had unfinished business with academia and an abiding love for all things Murdochian instilled in me by an elderly neighbour in my teens (I still wonder what I really made of *A Severed Head* aged 14 …)

We are all white middle-class women aged between 35 and over 50 (one chose not to give her age). Three of us have degrees, one completed part of an OU Humanities Foundation course and one is a trained Mental Health Nurse. While not completely ordinary, all being 'bookish', we are certainly not literature professionals and fit in nicely with Virginia Woolf's 'Common Reader', the educated but not scholarly reader who examines books for personal enjoyment.

4.1.2 Process

We started off reading and discussing one book per month until *The Nice and the Good*, after which we allowed two months per book. To structure the discussions, which followed a fairly traditional close textual reading format with which we were all fairly familiar from our studies, I had pre-formulated a list of themes to look out for. Murdoch is remarkable for the consistency of her themes, and doing this certainly allowed me an additional level of interest.

- Mysterious Characters (mysterious in origin, appearance etc.)
- Philosophers
- Jews & Irishmen
- London
- Women's Hair
- Magicians
- Institutions
- Theatres
- Large Men and Small Men
- Dualities / Pairs (similar and in opposition)
- Fate
- Confusing Relationships

We added as we went along

- Complicated plans (*Under the Net*)
- Farce (*Under the Net* to *Nuns and Soldiers*)
- Siblings (*Flight from the Enchanter*)
- Artificial Women (*Flight from the Enchanter*)
- Water (*Flight from the Enchanter*)
- Stones (*Flight from the Enchanter*)
- Dogs (later: Animals) (*The Sandcastle*)
- Saints (*The Bell*)
- Masks (became more solid as we progressed)

We had a discussion on these using a Yahoo Group, and once we had all had our say, I put together a post about the background to the book in question (critical reaction, Murdoch's recorded thoughts on the book, traceable models for characters and dogs).

4.2 Our reactions to the novels

Under the Net

We started off confused about how this novel caused Murdoch to be lumped in with the Angry Young Men of the period. One member of the group started to worry that she "took things at face value" and was not going to be good at the project. We identified plenty of Mysterious Characters, and London as being almost a character in itself in the novel. Some identified it as a farce, with misidentifications and comic capers. It was agreed that it was a brilliant and self-assured first novel.

The Flight from the Enchanter

All of us found it more complex than the previous book. Magic / enchantment and pairings and echoes started to become more important in the themes, and the themes started to become more important to the group as we negotiated our way through the read.

The Sandcastle

The group found this a more mature and 'believable' book. The mysterious gypsy character was enjoyed, as was the water theme. We started to notice that Murdoch uses a small range of hair styles in her work.

The Bell

Note: I will treat this in more detail in my discussion of the reading groups below. The group enjoyed the book but found some of the religious philosophy challenging. It was agreed that 'rebarbative' was the word of the book.

A Severed Head

Everyone noticed the fog and dream-like quality, with people appearing in each other's houses. The hair theme was as overt as usual, with a hair-cutting sequence again. There was a lot of talk of power and enchanters which we could see as a strong theme.

An Unofficial Rose

One reader loved how people's actions affected the other characters in a kind of web. The themes were less blatant and subsumed to the story, although Ali suspected some paedophilia again with Humphrey's actions. We loved that they drank some Lynch-

Gibbon wine at one point, referencing back to *A Severed Head*, the kind of detail you only notice when doing a fairly rapid chronological read. The grammatical constructions were noticed to be more complex: a more complex and subtle book overall.

The Unicorn

We found this to be a closed and incestuous system, obviously influenced by the Gothic. The musings on religion, guilt and goodness reminded us of *The Bell*. The themes, again, were woven in rather than 'all-pervading'. Duality loomed large, however, with the two houses and pairs of characters.

The Italian Girl

This was seen as "Very Murdochian, unhappy dysfunctional / odd family / group of people large house near water - all characters enchanted in some way with someone else". Goodness is key and mysterious characters abound, especially the Italian Girl herself. There is a hair-cutting and, as in *An Unofficial Rose,* art is playing a more major part.

The Red and the Green

Ali found this more of "a proper novel" as it is set in a recognisable time and place, although it still has Murdochian themes and characters. The sea is ever-present and there are plenty of enchanters. Gill thought "IM would have wanted to be Millie," a first comment of this kind on the books in the group.

The Time of the Angels

Several of the group found this one slow going and admitted to skimming the philosophical bits. Ali found the way in which characters gain access to each other's houses more realistic in this book and with the fog and London setting it was compared to several other of the novels. The Gothic side and isolation also reminded us of *The Unicorn*. Gill wondered whether the aim of her books was to discuss and get people to overthrow the underpinning institutions of society.

The Nice and the Good

The group enjoyed the mystery side of this novel. It had a "roundness, it came full circle," which appealed to Audrey. There was plenty of homosexuality and incest, hair and institutions. Had Murdoch recycled Fivey from Eugene in the previous novel, as they seemed identical-looking? The word 'rebarbative' also reappeared.

This was the point at which we moved to reading a book every two months instead of every month. The Baggy Monsters were approaching.

Bruno's Dream

Both Gill and Ali commented at this point that the books were becoming a bit 'samey', with Ali pointing out, "I do find myself saying to myself – 'oh yes the water thing, and then oh the hair thing, and here we go with the suicide thing' etc.". There are dreams and farce and a lot of watching and almost voyeurism. Echoes and dualities abounded and the dark, water and London were all prominent.

A Fairly Honourable Defeat

This was described as a page-turner and as being Shakespearean in its plots, with misleadings and overhearings. The relationships were so confusing that I was reduced to drawing a diagram in the back of the book. Again, this one was described as "a proper novel" but there was less discussion about it than about the earlier books.

An Accidental Man

London, yet again, was agreed to be a character in this novel. Institutions loomed large- schools, the army, the civil service, again as usual. The conversations in the book were found to be confusing and the group did not have much to say about it.

The Black Prince

This book polarised the group. It has always been a favourite of mine, and I enjoyed the layered narratives, metafiction and London setting. Ali found it so annoying that she threw the book across the room and did not finish reading it. Gill disliked it, too: "I didn't like it much, and I think one reason might have been the cleverness. If I hadn't known she'd written it, I might have thought someone had written it as a Murdoch parody". Given that only two of us finished it and one of us liked it, I neglected to write a 'Critical reaction' post on this book.

The Sacred and Profane Love Machine

There is plenty of hair and looking in to houses from gardens. Dogs played a huge part and dogs from other books were mentioned. The institutions of marriage, Oxford, church, school and army all get a look-in. There are many complicated relationships and lots of letters. Ali, thankfully, enjoyed this one very much.

A Word Child

Much magic and enchantment was found in this book which was universally enjoyed and appreciated for its setting and characters. I found that the relationships could be drawn in a kind of circle, which everyone appreciated. Gill thought that the characters could all represent different Tube lines with Hilary the Circle Line going around them all.

Henry and Cato

Lucy, who had recently joined the group, really enjoyed this one and was glad she had read a book she would not necessarily have read otherwise; she noted that there are fewer online reviews of this one than others. The balance of the duality was noted, two prodigal sons, and people loving others for their appearance rather than their real selves. People found the kidnap plot odd and somewhat farcical.

The Sea, The Sea

Various members noted with enjoyment the mention of Will Boase and Honor Klein from previous novels. It was Lucy's favourite of the ones she read but found it difficult to know what to say about it. The joy of youth and sadness of decline into old age were main themes for her, while Ali saw it as being about obsession and also found it too 'big' to write about well. Everyone liked the meals.

Nuns and Soldiers

Most were not gripped by this at the beginning but got drawn into it and found it exciting. The themes were very ripe and full in this one, we all felt. We liked the London pubs, Tim's time in France, and the power of Gertrude as the "pampered matriarch".

The Philosopher's Pupil

We all liked this one. Lucy praised Murdoch's ability to create a whole credible universe and suggested it could be made into a cult TV series like 'The Prisoner' with Murdoch fans visiting the real-life town upon which Ennistone is based. I see it as the perfect holiday read. The large chunks of philosophy did put off some of us, but that is part of the experience in the book, too, after all.

The Good Apprentice

Another one we all liked. Ali placed Seegard in Norfolk and never moved it from there. We liked the themes, particularly the supernatural touches, and we had an excellent discussion about being "good" but not actively so, and that not being enough, but the last word has to go to Ali: "got those two sisters mixed up – I sort of remember them as the nice but dim one who danced - and the weird one."

The Book and the Brotherhood

We all loved Grey, the Parrot, and the cat at Boyars. Lucy hated Crimond and found him unreal but loved Violet and Tamar; I found the opposite. This book contains one of the only scenes in Iris Murdoch to actually make me cry. Ali thought the huge number of people and relationships made her want to get to grips with them all right away.

The Message to the Planet

Sam said, "I didn't like all of the characters, but the ones I did like I was sort of rooting for. I also liked the intellectual ideas in the novel around 'received wisdom' gurus, allegorical links to religion and Christianity in particular." Lucy also liked it and found it amusing, loving Irina and her moustache and squint: Gill found it less believable than other books, and was "jolted" when she realised it was all about Christianity, and I have never liked it much.

The Green Knight

This was my second read and I very much enjoyed it and was relieved to find it stands up to a re-read. Lucy relished the "Murdochian theme of bad blood between brothers" and was "exhilarated and delighted" by it. We all liked the portrayal of Aleph, Sefton and Moy and the masked ball. And Sam found a whole slew of themes on just the first page (siblings, water, dog, London, duality, religion, and hair, if you count dog hair).

Jackson's Dilemma

All found it traumatic and upsetting. The writing had become more simple, the themes more bare. Maybe it should not have been published. It reminded Ali of the way the children she teaches write ("and then they did this, and then they did that") and inspired Gill, a speech and language therapy lecturer, to do some research of her own on Alzheimer's. I found it easier to read with the support of the others, and not as bad an experience as I had feared.

4.3 Case study questionnaire

Once I had decided to write up some research on the group, I conducted a brief questionnaire with the still-active members of the group – me, Ali, Gill, Lucy and Sam. This looked at what we all enjoyed and found difficult about the process, our favourite and least favourite books, and what we had got out of the process. A summary of the results of this follows:

Most of us had some knowledge of Murdoch's books, but all thought they would be intellectual and maybe daunting.

- As regards expectations, Ali was "looking forward to finding out about a giant of English lit" and we all agreed we wanted to see the development of Iris as a writer. Ali was worried that they would be a bit "deep" and whether she would be able to keep up. Lucy concentrated more on hoping that the other members of the group would be friendly, but not too keen and well-read. I, Ali and Gill were looking forward to sharing notes with other readers.

- How did we find the process? Gill found the first few less intellectual than expected, but some became "rather hard going". Sam felt a bit overwhelmed trying to catch up, but got over that. Gill enjoyed comparing notes, but felt her contributions became sparse at times. Lucy got a lot more out of the books by discussing them in a group, and I enjoyed sharing books I loved, although I had issues around being seen as the 'group leader' and 'expert'.

- Was it as expected? Gill found the books "quite light-hearted at times" and not as heavy as she feared. She took fewer notes as she went along, "wanting to read the books without having to intellectualise them". Ali found it a bit heavy going, especially the philosophy, but was surprised at how she liked some a lot more than others. Lucy found it easier and more inclusive than she had expected. Sam was defeated by 'A Fairly Honourable Defeat' but got back in her stride with 'The Black Prince'. Lucy found discussing themes "made the books come alive for me and I'm sure it made me read them with more attention and appreciation". I expected it to be more mutual and found it a little regimented, but the advantages outweighed the disadvantages.

- What was each person's favourite book?

- Sam: *The Message to the Planet* because "It had a plot with intrigue but was also centred on relationships".

- Ali: *A Word Child* ("I loved the characters, the London bits and generally the story"), *A Fairly Honourable Defeat* ("as it has the best vile character in Julius, and is unputdownable"; and *An Unofficial Rose* – "because I simply liked the world of that novel, the feel of it".

- Gill found it difficult because the books changed through time. She chose *A Word Child* or *The Philosopher's Pupil*, because they were "more optimistic" than some of the other novels, and had aspects that were different – "some of the novels felt a bit same-y".

- Lucy chose *The Sea, The Sea* as her single favourite, enjoying the gorgeous descriptions of nature and the "self-satisfied naughtiness" of Charles Arrowby. She also "loved the idea of a romantic heroine who was dowdy and ageing, it was so novel!" and found the ending, with

Charles' epiphany among the seals, "pretty perfect".

- Before I started the project, I would have said that my favourites were *The Philosopher's Pupil* and *The Sea, The Sea*. Afterwards, I would certainly add *A Fairly Honourable Defeat*, *The Book and the Brotherhood* and *The Green Knight*.

- The least favourite books were as follows:

- Ali – *The Black Prince* – "I didn't like the narrative voice, and the endless going over every little motivation, the constant analysing, etc."

- Gill – *The Black Prince* – "that seemed to be when she started using loads of totally unnecessary italics / quotation marks which really annoyed me – and there seemed to be more here than in any of the others".

- Lucy – it was *The Black Prince* but she re-read

it and it is now one of her favourites. But she expressed for all of us – *Jackson's Dilemma* – "I felt she'd already gone, by then, if you know what I mean. There was nothing in it of the old magic, for me."

- Sam – *A Fairly Honourable Defeat* – "Too many characters introduced at once and I found it difficult to have empathy with them … It didn't draw me in like the others and this led to irritation with the way that the characters reacted."

- Me – *Bruno's Dream* I disliked a little less this time around, but it is still not a favourite, and I do not like *An Unofficial Rose* although I cannot explain why.

• What did people gain from reading the books in chronological order? We all agreed that it showed Murdoch's development as a writer and enjoyed spotting old and new themes. Sam felt it allowed the books to become more accessible as time went on. Sam mentioned a feeling of "travelling along" with the author.

- And what did we get out of the process? I particularly enjoyed seeing my friends come to enjoy Murdoch and seeing their fresh approaches to books I knew so well. Lucy enjoyed the "stronger stuff" of the novels – despicable and bad behaviour. Gill enjoyed reading something "a bit more challenging than some of the stuff I read" and Ali similarly that it "helped to broaden [her] horizons". Lucy and Ali enjoyed reading books they would not have read before.

- Linking in with my book group research, they would all recommend reading Iris Murdoch to a book group, and most to friends, although carefully.

To sum up I would like to use Lucy's response:

"Despite Liz's analysis of Murdoch's influences and motives, Murdoch herself remains an enigma to me, a sort of androgynous intellectual giant, awe-inspiring rather than admirable! But I love her books passionately, and am heartened to find that in this age of alleged dumbing down, others do too. I would certainly like to participate in other Murdoch discussion groups after this experience."

4.4 The Reading group project: Conclusions

The reading group successfully made its way through all 26 of the novels, with one abandoned by one person of the three who attempted all of them. Although the group found its own voice and confidence in discussing the books and their own reactions, it did undermine the 'Death of the Author' thesis. This could have been down to my insistence on posting about critical reactions and writings on each novel, including information drawn from the chronology of Murdoch's life, as reactions were expressed to that, as I explain below.

It was interesting to note that one member of the group found the critical reactions that I gathered for each novel useful because it, "helps to put things in context with IM's life," which does seem to contradict my 'Death of the Author' thesis. However, it should be noted that this was early on, when discussing "Under the Net". Echoing this, in the reading of *The Sandcastle*, much was made of the relation of this more domestic novel to the time in Murdoch's life where she was considering settling down with John Bayley. By the time we had reached, *The Unicorn* and I had done my usual 'boring post' about the critical comments on the book, Gill had this to say: "I think it shows how she's developing as a person and an academic as well as an author. I'm enjoying the journey through her life".

Gill also liked to think about which characters Murdoch identified with, commenting that she would have liked to be Millie in *The Red and the Green* or "I think Iris sees herself as Morgan (or perhaps Julius, what a thought!)" when talking about *A Fairly Honourable Defeat*.

Ali made a powerful comment on her relationship as an individual reader to "The Academy" when she said, "I just suppose I feel that I have no reply to the academic stuff you've found for us – after all they know more than what I do".

5.0 THE BOOK GROUPS PROJECT: INTRODUCTION AND METHODOLOGY

5.1 Introduction

As discussed earlier, I had originally studied a group of people reading all of Iris Murdoch's work (see Chapter 4) then decided to stretch it out to cover other book groups.

5.2 Method

I used a self-selecting and partly snowballing effect to recruit book groups, advertising for participants through various groups and websites to which I belonged (emails to friends, BookCrossing, Facebook, Twitter, the IMS mailing list). I managed to gather 25 groups, all of which read *The Bell* and responded to a questionnaire I had formulated. This questionnaire was particularly interested in what a good book group book is considered to be, and whether *The Bell* fitted into that category, although there was room for general comment, too: I also took the opportunity to find out what people knew and thought of Iris Murdoch and her novels, which proved interesting.

I started off by researching book groups and the demographic information that I collected anonymously from my groups matched the general demographics found in such groups (middle aged, white women, who are fairly well-educated is a generalisation but a valid one), which makes my study of 25 groups based in the UK, US and New Zealand generalisable. One of my groups was a remarkably homogenous set of white ladies with degrees, retired and aged between 80 and 92!

Here I must briefly mention two 'pulls' or 'tugs' between the theoretical underpinnings of my work and the eventual methodology and process. Firstly, of course by transforming one simple reading group into a research project involving many more, I am perhaps transforming myself from a "common reader" into a scholar or even – shockingly – a critic. However, by taking an ethnographical position within the case study and remaining aware of my own presence as "expert", with the trials and tribulations that entails, I am facing up to that. And while Reception Theory and Death of the Author see the writer and reader as fundamentally disconnected, Murdoch as a public figure of course very much informs people's reactions to her even now. This, again, had to be faced up to squarely. But I found that, interestingly, although all of the groups mentioned That Film and Those Books, their stated reactions to the book, *The Bell* did not mention this foreshadowing at all, instead concentrating on those personal reactions predicted by the theory.

The 25 groups selected by a purposive and perhaps self-selecting process however did match book groups in the literature. There were 22 in the UK, two in the US and one in New Zealand.

The book group leaders were sent a questionnaire with questions on the group for them and some on Murdoch and the members' knowledge of her. Ethical considerations were covered by a statement for the leader and the groups stating their responses would be anonymised. All accepted this by email.

The book groups in my cohort were compared to book groups in the literature to check whether the results I gained would be generalisable – which would be more likely if they matched the demographic characteristics of the groups in the literature. Then I looked at what they knew of Murdoch to set the scene and to look at her heritage while I had the opportunity, what makes a good book group read, what they thought of *The Bell* and whether it was a good book group read, would they recommend it to other book groups or would they recommend it to other individual readers.

6.0 THE BOOK GROUPS PROJECT: RESULTS AND DISCUSSION

Note that not every group answered every question, or where choices were given, might have chosen more than one answer, so the answer numbers do not necessarily add up to 25.

6.1 Questions for the book group leader(s)

How did the book group form in the first place? Were you friends already, or did it form around a social group, location or other group of people?

The answers given broke down as follows:

Friends 5
Friends plus invitations 4
Academic group (U3A group, intervarsity group, New Zealand federation of university graduates, course on Shakespeare) 4
Library 3
Staff at a community organisation / coffee shop / charity shop 3
Work 1
Offshoot of another reading group 2
Marked as Not Appropriate (NA) 2

The literature says that reading groups tend to form from pre-existing groups of similar socio-economic background, 80% through informal groups that are not work or church related, so this was found to reflect the literature (Long, 2003). Literary groups, bookshops, academic groups were the main findings in Hartley (2001), but mostly neighbours and friends, and again, my groups reflected this. Long (2003) specifically said that groups form out of people at a similar life stage (in which we can include here groups with young families and the carers' group) or people with a similar background (which incorporates nicely my university groups). In fact, 56 of her 77 original groups formed without a church / other group tie, and this agrees to an extent with my 11 out of 22 groups who formed as part of friendship groups or as offshoots of other friendship-based book groups.

How many people usually attend the group? Is the attendance for this session similar to the usual number?

The answers were mainly between 6 and 12. In several cases, slightly fewer than normal were doing this special group read.

In Hartley's (2001) study, 77% of groups had between 6 and 10 members, which makes these groups generalisable in terms of size (Hartley's other groups commonly had 11-15 members, while some of the ones in this study had fewer than 6).

How often do you meet, at what time, and where?

The answers were as follows:

Monthly 19
Six-weekly 2
NA 3

And where they met:

Homes 10
Pub 4

Coffee shop / café 2
Library 2
Other community hall / charity shop / club 3
NA 3

This was not specified in the literature, although we can infer from the common friendship or library groups that the members in the literature would meet in similar places to these.

6.2 Individual questions (demographic profile)

Age / Gender / ethnic background / employment status / Highest level of education

Most groups (21) were extremely homogenous. I counted this as all within 10 years of age, same gender, same ethnicity, similar work profile, similar education levels.

For example, one group contained (32F White self-employed Master's / 29F White self-employed degree / 33F White employed master's / 36M white employed master's / 30F white Irish employed master's / 30F white employed master's – group of friends and colleagues), one described itself as, "We are retired professional women, white middle class, OAPs", and one amazingly homogenous group filled in their information as (80F white retired teaching / 79F white retired school / 77F white retired teaching / 71F white retired school).

Two groups were diverse in that one had one 20 year old student, the rest homogenous, and one was 20s-60s, with three ethnicities, a variety of work profiles and a variety of levels of education (note, this was a recently formed urban group of café customers that met at a coffee shop).

The literature says that groups are mainly women only or mixed – mine were more women-only than mixed (Long, 2003, Hartley, 2001). Hartley (2001) found that her groups were often of a small age range, for example one third were composed only of people in their 40s. This confirms the generalisability of these groups studied, with their low age ranges and uniformity. Twelve per cent of her groups had a wide age span, which is slightly more than in the groups under discussion here. As with Hartley (2001), ages here went up to the 80s. The average age in Long's (2003) groups was 51 and the average age of those of my participants who had answered this question matched this figure exactly. As for education, as Long (2003) and Hartley (2001) found, it was rare to find anyone not college-educated. Long's (2003) groups had 21% with a Master's or PhD. Regarding employment status, Long (2001) found that 67% of her groups had over half of their members in paid work, and my groups broadly reflected this, in that many of the retirees recorded their previous employment. In fact, more of my groups appear to have been working than Hartley's, perhaps because the phenomenon of book groups has spread further through the population since her study.

6.3 Books the groups read

Please list the books you've read over the last six meetings.

These were more varied than expected. The groups listed 129 books, of which 12 were duplicates or triplicates, so 115 individual titles.

Of those 129, 94 were from the 21st century, and 46 from 2009-11. The most popular were Christos Tsiolkas *The Slap* (3) Kathryn Stockett *The Help* (3) pairs of William Boyd *Any Human Heart*, Helen Simonsen *Major Pettigrew's Last Stand*, Kazuo Isiguro *Never Let Me Go* (film), David Nicholls *One Day*, Emma Donaghue *Room*, Rebecca Skloot *The Immortal Life of Henrietta Lacks*, Katherine Webb *The Legacy*, Andre Levy *The Long Song*, Kim Edwards *The Memory Keeper's Daughter*, Greg Mortenson *Three Cups of Tea*.

Did they include classics as well as these generally talked-about books? The range was more modern than expected. There was some Dickens, Chekhov, Steinbeck, Grass but then more "popular". Richard and Judy winners – 8 out of the 94 20th century books, so just under 10%.

However, the groups did evidence a strong pull towards winners and classics:

"We have selected groups of three books sharing a common theme; chosen from books who have been major (i.e. The Pulitzer, The Booker) prize-winners during a particular time frame. We are about to plan our next year's selection from the short-listed books from the Booker's inception in 1969 to 2008." – Bruno

"Our group always tries to have one classic in our requests each year. Our choices frequently are from recently published books or prize-winning titles." – Kitty, plus anecdotal evidence from people in other book groups suggests more classics. However, there were 23 groups reporting here with generalisable demographics.

The concentration on recent prize-winners over classics could be a reason for the lack of older books (from a non-UK group) "We debated here, and on previous occasions, why some of us struggle with an "older" book, and have discussed writing style on a number of occasions. Many of us enjoy contemporary books set in a historical time period, however seem to struggle with those written in that time period. As the only Brit in an American group, I seem to have less issue with this than the others, which we have also debated and maybe it is because of my academic / more classical education, and the books I was reading at school, both curricular and from suggested reading lists have exposed me to more "of the time" literature. The style doesn't seem so alien to me as it does to some of the others in the group, who like a hook from the first page (although personally I think the first line of this book is a good hook into the story!) and lots of dialogue from the outset." - Rozanov

There is a limitation here in that I only checked for Richard and Judy book club books because of time constraints.

The literature says that book groups tend to stick with the canon – classics then contemporary serious fiction and non-fiction, then good best-sellers, then genre. Literary awards and annual lists of notable books / Oprah and Richard and Judy are popular.

Researchers found that groups read contemporary fiction most, and some did talk about the canon (Long, 2003), with Hartley (2001) agreeing that they read moderns and classics.

6.4 Good book group reads

What makes a good book group read?

The answers were very wide-ranging here and were coded into the following headings:

Promotes discussion 21
Rich – lots of themes or ideas / depth of character 9
Challenges other people's attitudes / controversial 8
Outside comfort zone / Different 8
Relatable 4
Good writing 4
Come from a specific place or experience 4
Good story 3
Prize-winner / bestseller 3
Enjoyable / everybody likes it 3
Short 3 / (but not too short 1)
Social or political backdrop 2
Having reading notes and questions 1
Characters we don't like 1 (but one group disliked that)
Morally questionable behaviour 1
Ambiguous 1
Unknown with no preconceptions 1 (but one would

not like that at all)
Page-turner 1

To give some quotations from individual groups:

"One that makes a good discussion, e.g. a book with a twist or deep plot that we can talk about with each other. The book should inspire strong feelings. It isn't very useful if everyone liked it and if the book was too straightforward." – Franca

"A modern novel to appeal to the cross section of the group." – Midge (was this a clue to their picks?)

The literature says that a good book group book allows people to engage with the world and each other – a transformational process (Long, 2003) which is engaging. It is most important to find books that generate good discussions (Long, 2003). The most satisfying are to do with the moral world / dimensions and realism / character. It is important to read books outside what they are familiar with (Long, 2003). Good reading group books should affect the reader personally and challenge them to transform their life (Konchar Farr and Harker, 2008). The book does not have to be liked, but has to raise discussion and empathy and have characters (Hartley, 2001). "The book is expected to speak about the world" (Hartley, 2001). Franca's comment that "It isn't very useful if everyone liked it and if the book was too straightforward" echoes Long's (2003) groups stating that a book perceived as 'good' does not make a good book group read if everyone likes it and there is thus no discussion. Unlike Rooney's (2005) assertion about Oprah's book group's hegemony, the groups here are interested in more than the personal angle, although that is important to an extent. Hartley (2001, p. 76) found that her groups liked to read something they would not normally have read, and this was borne out with my group. Hers also stated that they did not necessarily have to like the book, again mentioned by the groups in the present study.

What's the best book you've read in the group recently?

Various books were mentioned (including, gratifyingly, *The Bell* four times) – most said because it had led to a good discussion or was controversial. Only three classics or older books were mentioned here, including "Tom Sawyer" by Mark Twain and "Two on a Tower" by Hardy. "The Slap" was mentioned once.

The literature did not cover this aspect specifically but it was useful to know that classics and modern books were mentioned equally, perhaps.

6.5 Group questions

Iris Murdoch

Had any of you read any Iris Murdoch books before reading The Bell?

One group answered yes
One group had one who answered no, with most yes
Six groups answered half and half
Twelve groups had one who answered yes, with

most no
Four groups answered no
One group answered specifically: "No: always meant to, never did" (Julius)

This does undermine A.S. Byatt's assertion that the charm has worn off Murdoch's works and no one is reading them any more (Turner, 2007, p. 115), however, I did not collect data on when participants had read the Murdoch novels they had read, so it is possible they were long-standing readers. However, the fact that 25 groups were willing to experiment with reading *The Bell* suggests that we can challenge that assertion.

What did you know about Iris Murdoch before this project?

Most groups had more than one answer here. We can split the responses into legacy engendered by the film and output about Murdoch, and those regarding her literary output, with a small sub-set of more personal knowledge:

Alzheimer's / dementia 12 dead 2
Husband (carer) 6
Film 16
Judi Dench 3
Kate Winslet 2
Jim Broadbent 1
Literary 9 (most included well-respected)
Intellectual 8
Irish 3
Sex 3
Oxford 1
Drinking 1
Controversial 1
Political 1
50s 1
Familiar 1
Has done a PhD on her / member of IM society 2
Has met her 1
Nothing 1

Some interesting comments were recorded:

"Since this project started we've all looked her up on the Internet." – Jesse

"Her books were perceived by some as including lots of sex and being a bit racy." – Marcus

"We all felt she is an author we "should have read",

feeling her work may have been suggested on school reading lists." – Rozanov

The concentration on Alzheimer's does echo Turner's (2007) assertion that Murdoch had become an "Alzheimer's poster girl", but the almost equal mention of her literary life, and supposed raciness and early life undermines the idea that this was at the expense of her literary reputation.

The book

Did you have any expectations of the book? Were you surprised?

Expectations:

Expectations varied widely but could be coded into groups and sub-groups:

Good – Cerebral / intellectual 7 or High expectations 7 or Well-written 1 or Like Du Maurier 2
Bad - Too hard 7 or Boring 6 or Worthy 3 or Dated 3 or Pretentious (because of intro) 1
Themes - Feminist 2 or Nature 1 or More on the bell itself 1

Nothing - Not sure 2 or No expectations 4

"With no prior knowledge of Iris Murdoch's work, a couple of the group had thought it might be more of a period piece, more along the lines of *A Room with a View*, and a couple admitted stereotyping the time period and expected more "pip-pip, what-ho!" as one of them put it." - Rozanov

Surprised by:

Surprises, again, could be divided roughly into good and bad, and also neutral, with some sub-sets and comments listed afterwards:

Good - More readable / enjoyable than expected 12 or More progressive 1 or Not dated 1
Bad - Dated 1 or Boring 1 or Didn't satisfy 1 - Not engaged with characters 1 - Expected more of a story 1 - Dense (language) 1
Neutral - Not feminist 1 - Intense emotion 1 - Homosexual element 1
Not surprised 4
"On reflection it was a brilliant story / I enjoyed it more than I thought I would" - Charles

"One person was very pleasantly surprised and has been turned into an avid Iris Murdoch fan (whilst before he had thought of her as a rather, heavy, boring and even parochial writer). Perhaps half the group seemed to find the book more readable and entertaining than they were expecting." – Edward

"I think most of us expected the book to be rather heavy going … more worthy than enjoyable … and we were surprised at how much we all did enjoy it." - Marcus

"It was a surprise that it didn't end as predicted". "I was surprised that I did not care for the book" – Ilona

"I was enthusiastic about the concept and setting but let down by the way in which she didn't come near to exploring their full potential." – Quentin

"We were all expecting this to be a difficult / hard read, to be erudite with obscure references, and we were surprised at how good it was to read, entertaining, challenging" – Sally

Although the groups did not self-identify as "non-academic" as Hartley (2001) found some groups doing, there was fairly clearly some concern about the 'hard' or 'academic' nature of the text, which was in some cases borne out.

Please summarise what you thought about the book. Did you all agree on it?

There were mixed reactions and lack of agreement (this is not necessarily a bad thing: as we have seen, book groups do not tend to like a book they can all agree on, or see it as a good book group read).

4 groups said all of the members liked the book (and this was a surprise for 2)
1 group reported that most liked it
2 groups had a complete mix
2 groups reported that most disliked the book
2 groups said all of the members disliked the book

I will now look at various aspects that were mentioned, with statistics and quotations drawn from the book groups' responses.

STYLE

Eight groups talked about the book being beautiful / well written: "One member commented that chapter ten, in which Toby goes for a swim, was so beautifully written that she read it several times, just for the sheer pleasure of the prose." - Willy

Three groups thought the book was wordy 3 (although one thought it would be wordy but it wasn't) and this could be off-putting

Four groups mentioned skill in descriptions – they could 'see' the place, but others mentioned being confused by descriptions or over-pedantic writing

Three groups mentioned the vocabulary. "When I started reading the book I found the sentence structure and vocabulary too sophisticated for me. I stumbled through some of the sentences, tripping up on much of the vocabulary used. I found myself having to re-read many of the sentences to grasp the full meaning of them, and this became slow and tedious. However, as I got further and further into the book, I focused more and more on the story (ignoring words I didn't know the meaning of) and concentrating on the story as it unfolded. By the end of the book I felt that I had enjoyed the story. Its setting, characters and events were very different from the books I normally read, and it is this that I particularly enjoyed." – Daisy

Four groups specifically mentioned the word "rebarbative".

There was no specific mention in the literature about style, although the expectations of wordiness which were not realised could come under reading books outside people's usual choices.

PLOT

There was much talk of the plot:

Six groups described the plot as surprising or having twists (one negative comment stated that it jumped around too much)
One group said the book was circular (but this was good)
Two groups speculated on the suicide

Four groups were disappointed and / or found the plot too convenient

Three groups found there was either no plot or it did not appeal: "An upmarket beach read" – Edward

Nicol (2007) asserts that readers enjoy Murdoch for the plots, as evidenced by the readers here, and that any complaints are to do with excesses in the plot, again evidenced here.

CHARACTERS

The characters were much discussed by the groups:

Two groups found the characters complex and appealing while one group found them shallow and three found there not to be any likeable characters.

Five groups felt Dora was their favourite character. Three groups disliked Dora: "Her emotions wore me out" – Ilona. The groups who discussed Dora said: Dora and Michael change, James, Paul and the Marks do not change – "Starting and ending with Dora, changed and improved whilst the others had slunk off" – Nigel. Dora reminded the Charles group of Princess Diana and Marianne Faithfull.

Two found Mrs Mark a pivotal although not necessarily favoured character. One group named the nuns as their favourite and two groups found Toby to be their favourite.

Three groups listed Michael as their favourite character. However, four groups disliked Michael or overtly described him as a paedophile: "One group member was fiercely anti him – regarding him as a dangerous and reprehensible paedophile who was (and would be again) a wrecker of lives – but at least one woman in the group said she had not even thought of him as a child abuser at all." – Edward

THEME

Themes found in the book were varied (suggesting a good book group read):

Eight groups named religion as a theme (for example, nuns versus confused lay characters / expectations of a religious life / what is Murdoch's view on religion?), although two found the sermons boring and skipped them.

Five groups identified a sex theme (it was racy / "What would Freud make of all this?" - Sally).

Four found a theme of contrasting world views.

Four groups mentioned a general gay theme.

Four groups mentioned paedophilia (e.g. predilection for boys, but using the term, too).

Three groups saw a theme of the microcosm: "Interactions of group within circumscribed time frame and confined setting enabled exploration of differing human qualities – innocence, goodness, weakness, evil, physicality, spirituality" – Bruno. "an exploration of the human condition within the microcosm of the isolated community" – Willy. "An adult fairy tale in an enchanted arena" – Midge.

Two thought the theme was about ethical choices, one said it was serious / philosophical and one went as far as to say it was a psychological thriller.

To link back to the literature, The book group literature mentions themes and areas for discussion, which were certainly found here. Nicol (2007) said the reader goes looking for themes and dualities, echoing what happens to the characters.

FEMINIST

One group each stated that the book was feminist or proto-feminist and discussed the roles of women in the book.

FUNNY

Four groups found the book funny or a farce (this was disliked by some). Marcus found it "very humorous in parts" while Quentin said, "The occasional slapstick scenes were appreciated by some and disliked by others" and Willy, "More than one member commented on how funny the book was – the black comedy of Procession Day was mentioned – and that other parts were comically absurd, even farcical"

DATED

The datedness of the book worked in two ways as

far as the groups were concerned. Some found it noticeable that areas that were shocking when it was written were no longer shocking; or contemporary terms are shocking *now*. Others pointed out that themes were discussed which were ahead of their time and brave.

Three groups stated that the book was dated in terms of the gay theme / sexual relationships being shocking at the time, not so much now. One group mentioned that attitudes had changed, (although perhaps not in the Anglican church) and one mentioned different treatment of mental health then and now.

Two groups talked of activities or vocabulary that was used then but are shocking now: drink driving, some phrases, vocabulary around being gay and making love. "Not politically correct very 1950s". One group found the long discussions seemed outdated and would not be appropriate now.

Three groups mentioned that the book was groundbreaking in covering controversial topics of the time

– homosexuality and bohemianism: "The early writing of homosexuality was exquisitely dealt with" – Jesse

Nine groups talked of how it was a snapshot of the 1950s or its time but not dated as such: "I'm glad I read it because it really showed what that time period was like and I could appreciate the difference between it and books written now but set in the past." – Franca; "A fantastically well drawn attack on the 'staidness' of English life and custom in the 1950s, as well as a great comment on the role of women at that point. Representative of a particular time and values that are recognised but in some ways alien which was fascinating." – Midge; "Suitable for our age group" – Kitty (the older group)

In one group, this aspect of the novel led to a discussion on when homosexuality in books became more acceptable, and another discussed writing style and contemporary versus older fiction.

The literature talks of good book group reads

engendering discussion, and this certainly happened here.

COMPARE

There was a small theme of what I called comparison in the discussions. One group mentioned that it was like Ian McEwan's fiction in its descriptiveness and turning on a single moment when the bell falls into the lake.

Several groups discussed the biographies, either discussing the value of the A.N. Wilson biography in general or, "I would suggest reading A.N. Wilson's biography of Iris Murdoch as a good antidote to John Bayley's writings about his wife" – Pinn

Three groups said it would make a good film.

This level of detail is not covered in the literature.

GENERAL

Finally, some general comments were made about

the novel:

Two groups reported that reading the book made them want to read more Murdoch (this one again or a different one). One member from each of six groups had or was planning to read more. Reports from the Franca group showed the members moving towards liking this author, almost against their will: "I would like to try reading other books by Iris Murdoch, as I really did like her writing, just not this particular book. / Now I see what all the fuss is about Iris Murdoch"; "We were very grateful to have been prompted to re-read it ourselves." – Bruno; "I have no doubt that some of us will read other books by her. I plan to re-read *The Sea, The Sea*" – Marcus.

Several groups mentioned the good discussion the book engendered: "We ended the session feeling there was much more to say – always a positive!" – Bruno; "General pleasure in the discussion and opportunity to read something we otherwise would have been unlikely to read" – Kitty; "The sort of book you would write an essay about" – Willy.

And finally, the Octavian group opined that *The Bell* "Needed a good murder".

Nicol (2007) asserts that the readers become immersed in the world of *The Bell*, looking for parallels, echoes and experiencing a similar journey through the novel as that of the characters, engaging with the conflict between the rational and irrational, the paired and repetitive structure and the themes, and noticing these overtly. My readers bore this out in their close and personal reading of the book.

Does *The Bell* make a good book group read? Why / why not?

Now we moved on to discussion about *The Bell* as a book group read. To the first question, does it make a good book group read:

16 groups said yes
7 groups had a mixed response
1 group said no

Why?:

I coded the reasons why as follows:

Discussion 17
Range of issues 3
Characters 3
Even though didn't like it 3
Plot 1
Controversial 1
Wanted questions 1

Why not?:

Too difficult 4
Not usual kind of book 2
No discussion 2
Characters hard to engage with 1
Unable to put into words 1

There was a good level of comment here from the groups:

"'The Bell' allows one to look at a different world that one doesn't often encounter and to think and talk about issues (sometimes 'difficult' ones) that one doesn't often have the chance to address." – Edward

"Most members like to be challenged by the book choice and appreciated that 'The Bell' challenged their preconceptions of what an Iris Murdoch novel would be like." – Willy

"Didn't think it was a good book group read until I started talking about it." - Julius

"There was a sense that we had all discovered something hidden and exciting (our own bell?!)" - Nigel

"I think it depends very much on the make-up of the group – many readers looking for more typical fare would not enjoy it." – Franca

"In general, I do believe there are books that stand the test of time; that are not classics; that are not contemporary and on the bestseller list, but are worthwhile book group reads." - Tallis

"Only adverse thought was that the homosexuality element or the religious elements could upset people who had strong views about either of these things." – Jesse

"Murdoch traditionally appeals to elitist and academic individuals and I'm happy with this. I think Murdoch could go the same way as John Cowper Powys. One of the warning signs of this for me is that the film about Iris Murdoch didn't really address her writing but was a love story." – Midge

"As a final thought I would add that it was one of the best meetings we have had, provoking much discussion, and we are likely to look at other 20th century authors who are no longer in vogue" – Marcus

If book groups read the canon (which may be flawed in this study), is Murdoch in it or outside? Turner (2007) talked about the modern canon as post-war, with Murdoch spanning academic and popular readers. Her reputation was at a peak in 1986-7, with *The Bell* an A level set text in the mid-80s. She seems for my readers to have slipped out of the canon – but then they do not read much of the canon anyway. Several groups or members will re-

read or read more, and it was noted that Murdoch is on some of the popular "1001 Books To Read" Lists.

Hartley (2001) recorded one comment about Iris Murdoch's work as having characters that the readers could not identify or sympathise with (p. 133), so clearly the groups in the present study were not alone in this. As a side note, since this was not a major theme, Hartley's (2001) research bears out the point that book groups do sometimes prefer to have questions on the book to work from.

Would you recommend this book and author to a) an individual friend b) another book group?

a) individual friend

6 groups said yes
14 groups had mixed answers
4 groups said no

More information was provided in the comments:

3 groups already had recommended Murdoch
5 said they would recommend but with limits
(religious / relevant 2 / quiet read / academics)

1 group said they would recommend it even though they didn't like it
2 would not because it is outdated
1 would not because it is religious

"One person has already recommended it to a friend and another had already finished another Murdoch book by the time of the discussion!" – Anax

b) another book group

14 groups said they would recommend the book to another book group
8 groups had a mixed response
2 groups said they would not recommend it

One group already had recommended it
Six said they would with limits (a group that liked academic criticism 2 / an older group / an established group / a religious group)
One said they would even though didn't like it
2 would not because it is outdated
1 would not because it is religious

Comments skewed it towards being a book group read: "It definitely needed discussion afterwards i.e. in a group setting." – Kitty; "We would recommend it to a book group as being a good example of mid 20C literature." – Pinn.

6.6 Addendum: the original book group's reaction to The Bell

I feel it would be useful here to summarise in more detail the original book group's reaction to *The Bell*.

The group, which was looking at different questions to those of the subsequent 25 reading groups, found themes of twins, siblings, doubling, contrasts (London / country, in particular), hair and mysterious characters. There was a great deal of religious philosophy, particularly in the sermons, love triangles, detailed plans.

The group was also interested in the theme of homosexuality, with an early comment from Ali summing this up: "Homosexuality - which I believe comes into other novels – a sign of the times of when the book was written IM has Michael "made" gay as a result of a seduction at school - is this a case of the abused becoming the abuser? Nick was only 15!!"

6.7 Conclusions

Many readers had heard of Iris Murdoch, most through the film, but some of the older members through her books, too.

The general initial impression was of a frighteningly intellectual writer whose books would be too hard. *The Bell* proved surprisingly readable, with a high percentage of readers enjoying it.

A good book group read is one that has a variety of characters and situations, characters you can identify with (this matched the general book group research) and plenty to discuss, including people of backgrounds other than one's own. It was generally agreed that *The Bell* matches these characteristics and so is a good book group read.

Most groups agreed they would recommend *The Bell* to another book group. Many groups / group members agreed they would recommend *The Bell* to a friend. Some members loved reading the book so much that they have gone on to read one or more other Murdoch novels.

Although Iris Murdoch is remembered for the film and her Alzheimer's, a refreshing number of groups did recall her literary heritage, Oxford, philosophy etc. Will be interesting to see if this balance shifts in the future (maybe this is an area for further study?).

In relation to Long's (2003) assertion that book groups function to "encourage groups toward critical appraisals of the social order" (p. xviii), this was borne out by the evidently lively discussions that some groups had on the representation of and attitudes towards homosexuality in literature and in society in general.

The readers generally enjoyed the book, sometimes in spite of themselves and prior expectations. The language, while challenging, was beautiful and the themes interesting. The location in terms of its time of writing was seen as an issue by a minority (from groups with a mainly 21st century reading habit).

Some of the reactions to the book surprised me.

There were several, in fact many, mentions of the "paedophilia" theme between Michael and Nick, with many readers sharing very strong responses to this. This can be related to Gadamer's ideas of "historical placedness" – reading a work through the lens of the current historical situation. There were also several mentions of some racist language, although most readers put that down to the time at which it was written. In general, more attention appears to have been paid to the homosexuality themes than the religious ones.

Although Pamela Osborn (2014) has read Michael as the powerful mover in the Michael / Nick relationship, I have always read it as being instigated by Nick, however maybe I am being led up the garden path (as one book group has it) by the manipulative unreliable nature. What I will say is that I believe the book to be being read through the lens of the current concerns about societal paedophilia, this aspect of the book thus being created by the reader in an echo back to reception theory, especially Jauss's (1971, cited in Abrams,

1993) assertion that the meaning of a book can change with successive generations of readers and the layers of history and readers that come between the text and its interpretation today.

7.0 CONCLUSIONS

7.1 Iris Murdoch and the common reader

We can compare the readers here with Long's (2003) readers confronted with Jane Austen, who found it difficult going, even when a "willing reader" (p. 180) and tended to reframe the discussion in terms with which they felt familiar – "she's very good on characterizations" (p. 182). I consider some of my groups to have relied upon this method for coping with the book – in the main, those who found the book "hard going"; they still reacted to the book, but tended to concentrate mainly on character and basic themes. But there were many more sophisticated readers who did engage with the book with interest and delight, and drew deeper themes and discussions from them. This is interesting in the light of the fact that my groups did echo the general make-up of groups in book group studies, so should have had similar reactions – in my personal opinion, the sermons in *The Bell* are no less difficult to read than sections of Austen.

The critics' readings of the book and the common readers' of necessity differed, with the critics taking serious and literary theory or feminism / theology based approaches and the readers a more personal approach. However, Nicol (2007) had talked about readers mirroring their experience in the book, and several authors discussed in the Critical Reaction section saw patterning, pairs and even Complicated Plans in the books which particularly my original book group had drawn out.

Book group members and the other ordinary readers found on LibraryThing had much in common, praising Murdoch for discussing homosexuality in a non-judgemental way at a time when it was illegal, concentrating on plot and character and pointing out dated sections. They both spoke of engaging with and caring for the characters. One reviewer wrote of child abuse but most talked of an affair or relationship: maybe there is more of a reluctance to openly use words like abuser or paedophile in what is effectively a public place linked to one's username, rather than in a private group with the guarantee of anonymity.

In a fascinating twist, while critical opinion might have been creeping towards an identification of minor abuse (no one published labelling it as paedophilia), several of the reading group members identified this theme in the book and seemed like they could not be persuaded away from it. This seems to have indeed led to the reader creating the novel, something which firmly echoes reception theory: seeing the book through the lens of popular culture and common contemporary concerns gave the readers a context in which they saw what the critics in the main have not seen. It will be interesting to view further critical opinions in the future, as maybe the critical lens will also revolve to take this into view.

7.2 Legacy

Regarding issues of legacy, it was interesting that, as Osborn (2014b) suggested in her discussion of works of mourning after Murdoch's death, the reactions of my book groups to her life and death were filtered through their reactions to the film and Bayley's books about her, rather than being direct personal reactions. A personal reaction was not mentioned even by those people who, like me, had been avid Murdoch readers before her death and up to her final output. However, their personal reading of the novel and of their own experiences into the novel perhaps echoes Osborn's assertion that mourning has become biography, with the living and the dead incorporated together, leading to a personal rather than objective creation of the dead person by the mourner. Obviously, reading an earlier book in Murdoch's oeuvre did not allow for a discussion of the mourning and death in novels such as *The Sea, The Sea* and particularly *Jackson's Dilemma*, with its heart-breaking final sentence.

7.3 General conclusions

In general, I have proved that Iris Murdoch is a writer for the 'ordinary' as well as the specialist reader – certainly for Virginia Woolf's 'Common Reader'. Although I approached the research from a 'Death of the Author' approach, there was a keenness from both the chronological reading group and the book groups to discuss the books in relation to Murdoch's life events and characteristics she was known for. It is perhaps impossible to read any book in complete isolation from its author. In the chronological group, interest was taken in the books as a whole and their relation to one another, and this was echoed in various comments I have heard over the years that people tend to be a fan of her oeuvre rather than a particular novel, although in the original group everyone had favourites and one book was discarded somewhat violently.

The canon and book choices

It was interesting to find that book groups in general relied on an authority to help them choose their books, whether that was the voice of tradition in the form of the canon or the voice of a popular but respected leader, such as Oprah Winfrey. This could have been a reason for the eager take-up of the project: I was initially surprised that an individual researcher could recruit so many book groups to read *The Bell*, but I can understand that I was acting as a form of 'authority' myself, hailing from what was perceived as the literary establishment: if I stated the book was worth reading, then it was worth reading. There may also have been some curiosity as to why this book was being included in a piece of research.[5]

Murdoch's need for her readers to enjoy the books on whatever level they wanted to enjoy them was borne out to quite a large extent.

It is refreshing and cheering to the researcher and those who read my text in manuscript that I was able to find 25 groups of people who were willing to read *The Bell*, and, indeed, have had interest and discussion about the project in my wider social circles which suggests that people are still interested in Iris Murdoch's novels as well as her life and decline.

Further research

In the light of my discovery of the 'authority' conveyed by asking the groups to read the book, it would be interesting to ask groups to read something significantly outside their usual genres, for example a science fiction or romance book, in order to judge a) whether the 'authority' of the researcher overcame the lack of approval from the canon in this case and b) what book groups would experience in such a reading.

[1] Pamela Osborn (2017) has perceived a link between Murdoch's work and Oprah, with this being the reason that particular Murdoch quotes are shared on Twitter, however neither of us know any more. Any information on this would be gratefully received.

[2] This situation is changing now – see Lovibond (2011), for example.

[3] I rely fairly heavily on Soule (1998) in this section, hoping he picked up the same themes I would have done. Any further information relevant to this research would be gratefully received.

[4] I have not found a direct mention of paedophilia in the context of *The Bell* in searches of the literature (although readers are welcome to correct me!). A search for the term and book title comes up with some blog posts from 2002 onwards and one document supposedly written by an active paedophile which I was uncomfortable to pursue further.

[5] Thank you to Pamela Osborn (2017) for this observation.

APPENDIX: THE READING GROUP THEMES

- Mysterious Characters (mysterious in origin, appearance etc.)
- Philosophers
- Jews & Irishmen
- London
- Women's Hair
- Magicians
- Institutions
- Theatres
- Large Men and Small Men
- Dualities / Pairs (similar and in opposition)
- Fate
- Confusing Relationships

We added as we went along

- Complicated plans (*Under the Net*)
- Farce (*Under the Net* to *Nuns and Soldiers*)
- Siblings (*Flight from the Enchanter*)
- Artificial Women (*Flight from the Enchanter*)
- Water (*Flight from the Enchanter*)
- Stones (*Flight from the Enchanter*)
- Dogs (later: Animals) (*The Sandcastle*)
- Saints (*The Bell*)
- Masks (became more solid as we progressed)

APPENDIX: THE BOOK GROUP QUESTIONNAIRE

Iris Murdoch Project QUESTIONNAIRE
For the book group leader

Thank you for volunteering your group to read Iris Murdoch's *The Bell*. There are four parts to the enclosed documentation:

1. An ethical statement about anonymity and an introduction to the project, for the group.
2. A few questions for you to complete in your own time.
3. A set of questions for you to submit to the individual members of the group. Depending on the group, you might like to print these out on slips, give the members slips of paper and ask them to write down the answers, or circulate a list. Please don't give me anyone's names. Please let me know if there were more members present than chose to fill in the details.

4. A set of questions for you to ask the group in the meeting in which you discuss The Bell. These are vague on purpose. Please give as much or as little information as you want to.

Once you've gathered this information, please return it to me in whatever format is easiest for you – you could type up a report, scan in your handwritten notes and email them to me, or ask for my address and post them to me.

Thank you once again for agreeing to take part in this study, and particularly for helping pilot the research and questionnaire!

For the book group members

Thank you for agreeing to take part in my Iris Murdoch project by reading *The Bell* and filling in my questionnaire. All of the answers you provide will be either anonymous in the first place (in the case of the individual profiling questions) or made anonymous (your group will be identified only by a code). I'm doing this research privately, without the backing of an academic institution, but the Iris

Murdoch Society is interested in seeing the results of this research project, and I may be able to publish a summary in their newsletter in due course.

Background to the project

The aim of this study is to find out whether Iris Murdoch's novel *The Bell*, is a good choice of book for a contemporary book group.

Reading about book groups and belonging to a few myself, I noticed that the books chosen tend to be either very recently published, especially when they're recommended by media outlets such as the Richard & Judy Book Club and various shop promotions, or classics, (e.g. Jane Austen and the like) or books that have been approved as classics by winning prizes (Booker winners, etc.). Some friends and I have recently been reading Iris Murdoch's fiction, and it struck me that one of her books might be a good book club read.

I've done some background research on book groups and how they choose what to read, and this bears out my original thoughts. I think there are many more mid-20th-century books that would be good book group reads, and have chosen a book by Iris Murdoch as an example, to see if this is so.

I'm now going to ask some groups of questions. One set will go to your book group leader(s) – that's to gather information about how your group formed, where it meets and what you've read in the past. Then there are some private questions, for each of you on your own (and completely anonymous) which will hopefully help me draw some conclusions if there are differences between groups and their thoughts on the book. Then there is a set of questions for you to discuss in the group. I want to stress here that there are no right or wrong answers, and you don't need to answer all the questions if you don't want to, although it would be great to have something down for all of them.

I hope you enjoy answering this questionnaire, and am very grateful to you for answering it for me! If anyone would like a summary of the research once it's finished, please send me an email address via your group leader, and I'll let you know the outcome.

QUESTIONS FOR THE BOOK GROUP LEADER(S)

These questions are aimed at giving me a background to the kind of group you are and the books you tend to read. Hopefully this will help me to see some patterns in people's attitudes to the book.

1. How did the book group form in the first place? Were you friends already, or did it form around a social group, location or other group of people?
2. How many people usually attend the group? Is the attendance for this session similar to the usual number?
3. How often do you meet, at what time, and where?
4. Please list the books you've read over the last six meetings.

INDIVIDUAL QUESTIONS (DEMOGRAPHIC PROFILE)

Please note that you do not have to answer any of these questions. You should not put your name on the sheet. I will only use this information to record the make-up of each group in terms of age, gender, ethnicity, employment and education, to see if I can see any patterns in the response of the groups I'm studying to the book.

1. Your age.
2. Your gender.
3. Your ethnic background.
4. Your employment status (employed full time / employed part time / self-employed / unemployed / retired).
5. Highest level of education you have achieved so far (including courses partly completed).

GROUP QUESTIONS

Iris Murdoch

1. Had any of you read any Iris Murdoch books before reading *The Bell*?
2. What did you know about Iris Murdoch before this project?
3. Did you have any expectations of the book? Were you surprised?

Book Group Books
1. What makes a good book group read?
2. What's the best book you've read in the group recently?

Iris Murdoch's The Bell
1. Please summarise what you thought about the book. Did you all agree on it?
2. Does *The Bell* make a good book group read? Why / why not?
3. Would you recommend this book and author to a) an individual friend b) another book group?

Any other thoughts

APPENDIX: THE BOOK GROUP CASTS THE FILM

Daisy: "We normally cast the book for a film, and the members wanted me to include this information, so here goes":

Dora - Renee Zellweger

Michael - Stephen Fry

James - Peter Bowles (when younger)

Nick - Jude Law

Toby - Nicholas Hoult

Murphy - Alice the dog (belongs to me)

Mrs. Mark - Dawn French

Mark Stafford - Sean Bean

Peter - Bill Oddie

Patchway - Clegg from Last of the Summer Wine

Mother Claire - Imelda Staunton

Paul - Alan Rickman

Noel - Hugh Grant

Mother Abbess - Judy Dench

ABOUT THE AUTHOR AND ACKNOWLEDGEMENTS

Liz Dexter is an independent academic and life-long Iris Murdoch fan. She is by trade an editor and transcriber, and has devoted seven years of her life to this study.

I would like to thank the Iris Murdoch Society, and in particular Anne Rowe, Frances White, Pamela Osborn and Miles Leeson for, respectively, their huge enthusiasm for the project, kind support and encouraging words, and two lots of photocopies at a stressful time near the end. Thanks to the lovely Carol Sommer and Rivka Isaacson for sharing presentation panels with me at the conferences. Rebecca Moden turned into a running-and-Iris-Murdoch friend and I am indebted to so many other members of the Society for their enthusiasm and kindness. Thank you to some of them for reading this for me: my mistakes are all my own.

Thanks of course to my original Iris Murdoch project readers and book groups.

And to my patient friends and family who have put up with the project and me going on about it, and of course to my then-boyfriend, now husband, Matthew, who has put up with the project, been presented to and even read some Iris Murdoch novels.

BIBLIOGRAPHY

Abrams, M.H. (1993) A Glossary of Literary Terms 6th ed. (New York, Harcourt Brace).

Abrams, M.H. (1993), A Glossary of Literary Terms 6th ed. (New York, Harcourt Brace).

Barthes, R. (1977) "What is an Author" in Image, Music, Text (London, Harper Collins).

Bellamy, M.O. (2005) "An Interview with Iris Murdoch" in Dooley, G., In a Tiny Corner of the House of Fiction (Columbia, S.C.: University of South Carolina Press).

Bigby, C. (2005) "Interview, 1979" in Dooley, G., In a Tiny Corner of the House of Fiction (Columbia, S.C.: University of South Carolina Press).

Brans, J. (2005) "Virtuous Dogs and a Unicorn" in Dooley, G., In a Tiny Corner of the House of Fiction (Columbia, S.C.: University of South Carolina Press).

Byatt, A.S. (1994) Degrees of Freedom (London, Vintage).

Conradi, P. J. (2010) Iris Murdoch: A Writer at War: Letters and Diaries, 1939-1945 (Short Books).

Conradi, P.J. (2007) "Existentialists and Mystics" in Rowe, A. (ed.) Iris Murdoch: A Reassessment

(Basingstoke: Palgrave Macmillan).

Dooley, G. (2003) From a Tiny Corner in the House of Fiction: Conversations with Iris Murdoch (Columbia, S.C.: University of South Carolina Press).

Fish, S. (1980) Is there a Text in this Class: The Authority of Interpretive Communities (Cambridge, MA.: Harvard University Press).

Gordon, D.J. (1995) Iris Murdoch's Fables of Unselfing (Columbia, University of Missouri Press).

Hartley, J. (in association with Sarah Turvey) (2001) Reading Groups (Oxford: Oxford University Press).

Hobson, H. (2003) "Lunch with Iris Murdoch" in Dooley, G., In a Tiny Corner of the House of Fiction (Columbia, S.C.: University of South Carolina Press).

Holub, R. (1984) Reception Theory: A Critical Introduction (London: Methuen).

Horner, A. and Rowe, A. (eds.) (2015) Living on Paper: Letters from Iris Murdoch 1934-1995 (London: Chatto & Windus)

Iser, W. (1978) The Act of Reading: A Theory of Aesthetic Response (London: Johns Hopkins UP).

Konchar Farr, C. and Harker, J. (eds.) (2008) The Oprah Effect: Critical Essays on Oprah's Book Club (New York: State University of

New York Press).

LibraryThing (2017) "Iris Murdoch, The Bell" [reviews] www.librarything.com [accessed 27 July 2017]

Long, E. (2003) Book Clubs: Women and the Uses of Reading in Everyday Life (Chicago: University of Chicago Press).

Lovibond, S. (2011) Iris Murdoch, Gender and Philosophy (London: Routledge).

Martin, P. and Rowe, A. (2010) Iris Murdoch: A Literary Life (London: Palgrave).

Morgan, D. (2010) With Love and Rage: A Friendship with Iris Murdoch (Kingston: Kingston University Press).

Murdoch, I. (2003) "Interview, The Times" in Dooley, G. In a Tiny Corner of the House of Fiction (Columbia, S.C.: University of South Carolina Press), p. 15.

Myers, J. (2003) "Two Interviews with Iris Murdoch" in Dooley, G., In a Tiny Corner of the House of Fiction (Columbia, S.C.: University of South Carolina Press), p. 230.

Nicol, B. (2007) "The Curse of The Bell: The Ethics and Aesthetics of Narrative" in Rowe, A. (ed.) Iris Murdoch: A Reassessment (Basingstoke: Palgrave Macmillan).

Noble, E. (2010) The Reading Group (London: Penguin).

Osborn, P. (2014a) "'Robbed of Thy Youth by Me":

The Myth of Hyacinth and Apollo in The Bell," in Luprecht, M. (ed.), Iris Murdoch Connected: Critical Essays on her Fiction and Philosophy (Knoxville, University of Tennessee Press) p. 85-96.

Osborn, P. (2014b) "Afterword: The Mourning of Iris Murdoch (and How She Survived it)" [abstract], paper presented at the 2014 Iris Murdoch Society Conference (12-13 September 2014).

Osborn, P. (2017) Private electronic communication after reading the manuscript of this study.

Rooney, K. (2005) Reading With Oprah: The Book Club that Changed America (Fayetteville: University of Arkansas Press).

Silverman, D. (ed.) (2011) Qualitative Research: Issues of Theory, Method and Practice (3rd ed.) (London: Sage).

Soule, G. (ed.) (1998) Four British Women Novelists: Anita Brookner, Margaret Drabble, Iris Murdoch, Barbara Pym: An Annotated and Critical Secondary Bibliography (Scarecrow Press).

Spalding, T. (2012) Private communication via Twitter, October 2012.

The Book Group (2002) TV Series, Channel 4 (2002-2003)

Thomas, G. (2009) How to do your Research Project (London: Sage).

Todd, R. (2005) "Encounters with Iris Murdoch" in Dooley, G., In a Tiny Corner of the House of Fiction (Columbia, S.C.: University of South Carolina Press).

Turner, N. (2007) "Saint Iris? Murdoch's Place in the Modern Canon" in Rowe, A. (ed.) Iris Murdoch: A Reassessment (Basingstoke: Palgrave Macmillan).

Viner, B. (2013) "Great British Institutions: The Book Club", The Telegraph, http://www.telegraph.co.uk/culture/books/9937708/Great-British-Institutionsthe-book-club.html

White, F. (2014) Becoming Iris Murdoch (Kingston: Kingston University Press).

Woolf, V. (1925) The Common Reader, First Series (London: Hogarth Press).

Made in the USA
Columbia, SC
15 August 2017